The
HEALING
TOUCH

A GUIDE
TO HEALING
PRAYER *for*
YOURSELF AND THOSE YOU LOVE

NORMA DEARING

Chosen Books
A Division of Baker Book House Co
Grand Rapids, Michigan 49516

The
Healing Touch

© 2002 by Norma Dearing

Published by Chosen Books
A division of Baker Book House Company
P.O. Box 6287, Grand Rapids, MI 49516-6287

Printed in the United States of America

Library of Congress Cataloging-in-Publication Data

Dearing, Norma, 1952–
    The healing touch : a guide to healing prayer for yourself and those you love / Norma Dearing.
        p.   cm.
    Includes bibliographical references and index.
    ISBN 0-8007-9302-1 (pbk.)
    1. Spiritual healing. 2. Prayer—Christianity. I. Title.
BT732.5 .D37 2002
234′.131—dc21
                                                  2001047432

For current information about all releases from Baker Book House, visit our web site:
http://www.bakerbooks.com

This book is dedicated to
the late Reverend Frank P. Dearing
and
Francis S. MacNutt, Ph.D.

*I thank God for the privilege
of going alongside two such holy
men in the healing ministry and
learning from them the love
of Christ and the power
of God's healing touch.*

CONTENTS

ACKNOWLEDGMENTS

Writing this book was not easy for me. It was actually more painful than pregnancy and childbirth, since it took three times longer and I received no drugs. As a total extrovert, I would rather be speaking in front of ten thousand people than sitting alone behind a computer writing one page. When I felt God calling me to share my knowledge of the healing ministry in book form, I replied, "I could never do such a thing without grace and discipline sent straight from above!" His response: *Yes, that's what I had in mind.* My first acknowledgment must be to the Lord for giving me the strength and discipline to complete such a daunting task.

There are so many others He used to encourage and help me with this project:

Grace Sarber, my Jacksonville editor, whose love, encouragement and eye for detail helped prepare a manuscript I was proud to offer for publication; Beth Hobby, who lovingly typed this manuscript, donating a brand-new computer to *The Healing Touch* in the process; my wonderful husband, Peter Dearing, who demonstrates the love and grace of Christ to me each and every day; Ann Bauwens, for her prayers, typing and computer skills, and belief that I "can do all things through Christ who strengthens me"; my parents, Reba Wade and the late Preston Wade, whose honesty and dependability taught me to expect the same from my heavenly Father; my children, David and Vicki Dearing, James and Mandy Matti, Shelley, Jason and Danny Dearing, as well as my adopted daughter, Katie Bauwens, for their unlimited encouragement and help with the computer at all hours of the day and night; my faithful prayer partners and intercessors, Sue Wilkinson, Barbara Newman, Betty Heindel, Audie Hall, Don Harvey, Joy Lamb, Edie Whitaker and Jane Wilson; David Busse and the Board of Trustees of Impact Communications Ministries who love and support me unconditionally; the prayer ministers at Christian Healing Ministries; the many people whose stories are represented in this book; Jane Campbell, editorial director of Chosen Books, whose personal encouragement and belief in this book made it a reality; and Ann Weinheimer, my editor, whose expertise and professionalism created the finished product. To each and every one of you, thank you. May God continue to bless you with extraordinary gifts and talents.

FOREWORD

Norma Dearing is a very gifted woman. For fourteen years she worked with us as director of prayer ministry at Christian Healing Ministries in Jacksonville, Florida, where she exercised several wonderful, God-given gifts. You will see these in evidence in this fine book.

In the first place, Norma is a gifted prayer minister who took a very real personal interest in the wounded people who came for prayer. For her it was not so much a task as a deeply felt mission. She has a big heart and concern for sinful, hurting humanity—and that includes all of us, doesn't it? Whenever anyone with a particularly difficult problem came to CHM, especially if he or she needed inner healing, Norma would be the person we wanted to take it on. Once she started praying with a person, she would loyally stay with them, often for years (see Cindy's story at the end of this book). Consequently, Norma writes out of a wealth of practical experience. She does not propose easy answers or magical solutions, but offers solid teaching that leads to practical, realistic prayer for healing.

Norma began her involvement in the healing ministry more than twenty years ago by learning from her beloved father-in-law, the late Father Frank Dearing, a pioneer in the healing ministry as a pastor in the Episcopal Diocese of Florida.

He learned to pray for the sick long before it was the accepted practice that it has now become. He never really retired because even when he was in his seventies and eighties, a stream of people kept coming to him for counsel and prayer in his home.

To what she learned from Father Frank and others, Norma has added what she has gained from her own experience. Since she has worked patiently for years with victims of deep wounding and sin, Norma makes practical suggestions in this book that you will not find in the books of healing evangelists who necessarily deal with large crowds and cannot spend much time talking and ministering one-on-one with individuals.

Since she has spent hours—often years—with her clients, she has learned how to pray with people who need layers of in-depth healing over a long period of time. Since Norma is approachable, hurting people open up to her, and these hundreds and thousands of clients give Norma a wealth of fascinating stories to illustrate her teaching, such as those you will find here.

Along with her loving gift for ministry, Norma possesses an enthusiastic ability to teach. She has a creative gift for making her teachings practical and down-to-earth, so that you will find in these pages many suggestions and prayers for all kinds of situations in which you may find yourself.

The Healing Touch will, I believe, be a valuable addition to anyone's healing library, for several special reasons.

First, Norma incorporates topics that do not appear in most books on healing, but which are very important and belong to the healing ministry in the deepest sense. She writes chapters, for example, on healing our relationship with God, on salvation and on generational healing. These are special aspects of healing, often neglected but truly important.

Second, because of her wide experience of spending time praying with people with the deepest problems—the kind not often addressed in large healing services or by praying for a short time after Sunday services in church—she has written chapters that I personally found most helpful, such as how to pray with people suffering from sexual problems and being cut free from various ties.

I trust that you will find, as I did, *The Healing Touch* a most welcome and valuable addition to your library and that it will help you to grow closer to our Lord.

FRANCIS S. MACNUTT, PH.D.
CO-FOUNDER AND PRESIDENT
CHRISTIAN HEALING MINISTRIES, INC.
JACKSONVILLE, FLORIDA

HEALING

OUR
RELATIONSHIP
WITH GOD

ONE

GOD'S PERFECT PLAN
FOR WHOLENESS

From the very beginning of time, God desired for us to be healthy physically, emotionally and spiritually. As an integral part of this perfect plan, God also established the idea of relationship with His created children. He wanted intimate and unbroken communion with each one of us individually that we might walk in the peace and protection of His will. And, of course, He wanted us to live in healthy relationships with one another.

He showed His inexpressible joy in our arrival by creating a beautiful world for us, one warmed by the sun in the day and guided by stars at night. He spoke into being plentiful waters to refresh us, land with vegetation for food, and animals that He allowed Adam to name. All of this He gave to us, and He gave us dominion over this world as well.

So God created man in his own image, in the image of God he created him; male and female he created them. God blessed them and said to them, "Be fruitful and increase in number;

fill the earth and subdue it. Rule over the fish of the sea and the birds of the air and over every living creature that moves on the ground." Then God said, "I give you every seed-bearing plant on the face of the whole earth and every tree that has fruit with seed in it. They will be yours for food."

GENESIS 1:27–29

God gave Adam everything he could possibly need to live an abundant life—beauty around him, food, trust to care for His creation and even a helpmate to enjoy it with him. All of these were wonderful, yes, but most importantly Adam had a loving, open, direct and personal relationship with God, our Creator. He was able to communicate with God, fully secure in the knowledge that he belonged to Him.

There was only one prohibition: "And the LORD God commanded the man, 'You are free to eat from any tree in the garden; but you must not eat from the tree of the knowledge of good and evil, for when you eat of it you will surely die'" (Genesis 2:16–17).

During this time, Adam had no knowledge of good versus evil. He saw everything in his life as good and holy and pure. Adam experienced only love, joy, peace, goodness and kindness. Can you imagine what this would have been like?

I get a tiny glimpse into the Garden of Eden by watching my grandson, Andrew. He has total trust that his parents will care for his every need. At five years old, he has no idea that he lives in an evil and perverse world. He enjoys a safe home environment, with good things to eat and toys with which to play. Thanks to the Lord's blessing, his parents even produced a little sister for a playmate.

This feeling of love and security is what Adam and Eve enjoyed in the Garden before they chose to disobey God and eat the forbidden fruit.

The Bible makes it clear that Satan is our enemy. He is always crafty in the ways he works to separate us from God. For instance, he never tells us directly to disobey or disrespect

16

God; rather he fills his lies with just enough of the truth to ensnare and confuse us. Look at how he tempted Eve:

> "You will not surely die," the serpent said to the woman. "For God knows that when you eat of it your eyes will be opened, and you will be like God, knowing good and evil."
>
> GENESIS 3:4–5

Eve fell into the trap. Suddenly she desired the wisdom and knowledge that she believed the tree could give her.

It certainly gave her knowledge. After sharing the wealth with Adam, they both had knowledge. They had the knowledge of good and evil, something from which God, in His infinite wisdom, wanted to protect them.

By disobeying God in this simple act, Adam and Eve separated themselves—and thus all of mankind—from Him. The intimate relationship they had enjoyed with God was now severed. They could no longer commune with Him as they had done previously. This separation, known as sin, has affected every generation that followed.

The entry of sin into God's beautiful world not only brought sickness, pain and torment to His people but grieved Him greatly. God continued to long for a close and personal relationship with *all* of His people.

This seemingly hopeless situation was one that only God could fix, and He did it in a very special way. Only one Person could restore the relationship between God and man: His Son, Jesus Christ.

Why Did Jesus Come?

Why did Jesus come? First and foremost, Jesus came because God sent Him. God's people were having a difficult time connecting with Him and knowing His love for them. Only a few special people, Old Testament luminaries such as

17

Abraham and Moses, could communicate with God. Thus, God sent His Son, Jesus, to the earth—God-incarnate, fully divine and fully human—to exhibit divine love and to enable *all* of God's people to have a direct and personal relationship with Him. Even Jesus' name, which means "God with us," bears testimony to the fact that the heavenly Father reached out to us through His Son in order to reestablish that relationship. At God's bidding Jesus became the bridge across the river of sin that separated man from God.

God made two specific things about Jesus' coming and going quite extraordinary. First, He was conceived by the power of the Holy Spirit and born of a virgin. Second, after His death He was resurrected bodily and Satan's hold over death was broken. Definitely not your usual entrance or exit!

Until Jesus' victory over sin and death, the world could not relate to God on a human level. The average person had no chance of communication with God, nor any hope that God could understand human suffering. The incarnation, death and resurrection of Jesus changed all of that. Mankind could now express his concerns to God directly and expect God to empathize with his pain. Through the sacrifice of His Son, God redeemed His creation and entered once again into relationship with us.

The concept of God as Father can be difficult for some who see this role in a negative light. For example, a person who has a difficult relationship with his earthly father may experience fear when trying to know God as heavenly Father. One of the main missions of the Son was to reveal the true nature of the Father.

In the gospels of Matthew, Mark and Luke, God is referred to as Father more than fifty times. In John's gospel, a book that speaks so much of relationships, God is referred to as Father 87 times.

Jesus Himself said, "All things have been committed to me by my Father. No one knows the Son except the Father, and no one knows the Father except the Son and those to whom the Son chooses to reveal him" (Matthew 11:27). Thanks to God's amazing grace, we are all able to receive the revelation of God's love and through Jesus be reconciled to Him. Knowing Jesus allows us to know God's love.

Another reason that Jesus came was to express that love in tangible ways. He did this by healing the sick and proclaiming that the Kingdom of God is at hand.

In other words, empowering Jesus to heal was an expression of God's loving desire to relate with His people at the level of their most basic needs.

Every place Jesus traveled, the first thing He usually did was heal the sick or cast out demons, basically another form of healing. Then after getting people's attention, He proclaimed that "the Kingdom of God is at hand." There were times that He proclaimed the Kingdom of God first and then healed. Either way, the message was clear that God's healing power was at the very core of His plan.

Jesus' coming fulfills the prophecy written in Isaiah 61:1: "[The Lord] has sent me to bind up the brokenhearted, to proclaim freedom for the captives and release from darkness for the prisoners." Many who need physical and emotional healing have been held captive by the enemy. Jesus came to destroy the works of the devil and set us free: "He who does what is sinful is of the devil, because the devil has been sinning from the beginning. The reason the Son of God appeared was to destroy the devil's work" (1 John 3:8).

Another reason that Jesus came to earth was to initiate the work of the Holy Spirit. When Jesus returned to the Father after His resurrection, the Father sent the Holy Spirit to dwell in and with mankind as guide, comforter and enabler. This was the second great "commissioning" from God to His creation. With the gift of the Holy Spirit, we now recognize the complementary roles of each Person of the triune Godhead in establishing and building relationship with us.

All of these are important reasons why Jesus came, and the concept of Jesus as healer is the foundational focus of this book, but we must never lose sight of the most important reason that He came: He came to be our *Savior.*

Paul writes:

> For God was pleased to have all his fullness dwell in him, and through him to reconcile to himself all things, whether things on earth or things in heaven, by making peace through his blood, shed on the cross. Once you were alienated from God and were enemies in your minds because of your evil behavior. But now he has reconciled you by Christ's physical body through death to present you holy in his sight, without blemish and free from accusation.

Colossians 1:19–22

Jesus came as the redeemer of our mistakes and our imperfections. He came as the sacrificial lamb for our sins, so that we might have the opportunity to live with Him forever. If we are able to face the truth about ourselves, we know we are guilty. We know that we have sinned and deserve to die.

Imagine for a moment that you are facing a firing squad. You have committed crimes and you deserve to be punished. You are blindfolded and waiting for the shots to ring out. You hear footsteps coming toward you. You are not sure who it is, but there seems to be a hush among the executioners.

Someone begins to untie your hands and take off the blindfold. You open your eyes, blinking and trying to focus on who is standing before you. You then realize it is a man, but not just any man. It is Jesus, the Son of the living God. He looks at you with great love and compassion, even though He knows everything there is to know about you. Finally He speaks, saying, "Run along now. I will take your punishment for you."

This is *grace,* pure and simple. We cannot earn it and we will never deserve it.

Years ago, while taking part in James Kennedy's Evangelism Explosion Program, I learned an acronym for the word *grace* that I will never forget: *God's Riches At Christ's Expense.* This is truly the best definition of grace I have ever heard.

Grace is a difficult concept for many to grasp—even for pastors or lay people in longtime Christian work. It does not relate to the attitude prevalent in our society, the attitude of performance orientation. We are programmed from preschool to expect that if we perform well we will be rewarded. Think about those "happy face" stickers and gold stars we enjoyed earning. These are important tools, I agree, but by experiencing such a system of reward and punishment many people, especially in the United States, have trouble moving past the idea that nothing in life is free. We have to earn our way. We hope to earn God's favor by praying harder or performing enough good works. This makes it difficult to grasp the idea of grace.

Most times, anything that seems too good to be true probably is.

There is, however, one exception: the grace of God. God's grace is a free gift, and all we need to do is accept it. Scripture makes this clear: "For it is by grace you have been saved, through faith—and this not from yourselves, it is the gift of God—not by works, so that no one can boast" (Ephesians 2:8–9).

Over the years many people have said to me, "Well, I'm not worthy, I'm not worthy." I always respond with the same answer: "You're right, you're not. You're not and I am not. Even Billy Graham isn't! No one is."

Remember the words of John the Baptist at the river Jordan: "I indeed baptize you with water unto repentance: but he that cometh after me is mightier than I, whose shoes I am not worthy to bear: he shall baptize you with the Holy Ghost, and with fire" (Matthew 3:11, KJV).

Why did Jesus come?

He came because we were not worthy. We were not good enough or holy enough, and we never will be. Because we were not worthy He came to die in our places. It is only as we

21

recognize this and accept His worthiness and His grace that we are able to spend eternity with Him.

A man died and went to heaven, and Saint Peter met him at the gate. Saint Peter said, "Welcome to heaven! It's going to cost you one hundred points to come in. Tell me about your life."

The man thought for a few minutes, and then he answered confidently, "Well, I have gone to church my entire life. I was raised in the church, and I even attended when I went away to college."

"That's wonderful," Saint Peter replied. "One point."

The man was startled by this response, but he continued. "Well, I not only attended church, but I was active. I served on the vestry for several terms. And, of course, I tithed. This was a special requirement for serving on the vestry, but I would have tithed anyway.

"Oh, and one of the most important things I did was teach the eleven- and twelve-year-old boys' Sunday school class. They were a rough group, and nobody else could really handle them."

Saint Peter had been listening intently and with a big smile he said, "Wonderful! One point!"

The man began to worry. Breaking out in a sweat, he continued, "Well, I tried to be a good person. I never really cheated on my income taxes or anything, and I think I was a good husband and father. I mowed the grass for the little widow lady who lived next door. And if I couldn't do it, I made sure my son did it for her."

Saint Peter smiled and said, "Very good! One point!" After this, the man could not think of another thing to say on his own behalf. So, feeling hopeless, he turned away dejectedly and muttered, "Man, there's no way to get into here except by the grace of God."

Saint Peter responded with a big smile, "Ninety-seven points! Come on in!"

The only way that we can get to heaven is through Jesus. Now, having restored our individual relationships with God, Jesus shows us the way: "I am the way and the truth and the life. No one comes to the Father except through me" (John 14:6). It is what Jesus did for us that counts, not our good works or the churches we attend or the families into which we are born. It is what Jesus did for us and it is absolutely free. This is why He came.

Communication with God

Once we understand that we may enter into relationship with God, we have a choice. How will we respond to Jesus' invitation?

Scripture teaches us that before we were formed in our mothers' wombs, God knew us; He even knows the number of hairs on our heads (see Luke 12:7). He created us in love. He has restored us to Himself. He longs to communicate with us. And in His great love, He leaves the final decision up to us: He allows us the free will to choose whether to be in relationship with Him or not.

Perhaps we were born into a Christian family and it seems natural to know Him. Perhaps through nature we came to the realization that a higher being had to create so much beauty. Perhaps we cried out during a crisis and felt the peace that only His presence can bring.

Somewhere along the way we came to the realization that something out there is much larger than we are, and that we are not only connected to it but can have intimacy with it. We are actually able to communicate with this God of the universe. What a stunning revelation!

In the mid-1980s our family moved to England for a year to do missionary work. While there my husband and I were involved in an evangelism street ministry called Open Air Campaigners. We were part of a team that went into towns on busy shopping days, set up "paint boards" on which we drew pictures, and told stories to whoever stopped to listen. We talked about feelings and events that the secular world could relate to such as depression, worry and finances.

After about four minutes of story and pictures, we told the listeners about Jesus and how He could help in these various situations. We then handed out little books about Jesus and offered to talk with them about any concerns or questions they might have. We were amazed that year at the hundreds of people who answered the call of Christ right there in the street while they were out shopping.

We also learned that our train trips into London, which took approximately forty-five minutes, were opportune times to converse about the exciting things happening with the street ministry. It was interesting to watch reserved Englishmen hold their newspapers and books in place but not turn a page for thirty minutes because they were listening. Often people would begin to ask questions about our faith and how they could know Jesus. It was on one of these trips to London with my friend Denise that a British rock star first answered the call of God.

On this particular day no seats were left in the coach section and we were allowed to sit in first class. We were disappointed initially because no one else was in the compartment, but we decided that the Lord did not have anyone for us to talk to at that time. After all, we had prayed before boarding to be led to the right place and situation.

Denise suggested that we share with one another the things that the Lord was showing us in our own lives. About this time, a handsome young Englishman entered the compartment wearing a business suit and sporting a gold earring. His long hair was pulled back in a ponytail. We said hello and continued our conversation. He began to read his book.

We noticed as we talked that our riding companion had not turned a page in a long time. Eventually, he said, "Excuse me, I can't help but overhear your conversation. I wonder if I might ask you ladies a few questions?"

"Of course," I answered, being the more extroverted one. I knew that Denise, who is a mighty prayer warrior, would be more comfortable with my talking and her quietly interceding.

He proceeded. "I know this may sound strange to you ladies, but I feel as though God is calling me. My name is Alvin Stardust and I'm a pop singer. I've made some mistakes in my life, but lately it just seems that God is kind of speaking to me in different situations, actually as though He's calling me. Does this make any sense?"

I responded, "Yes, it makes sense. God does communicate by calling us, sometimes using very specific and individualized circumstances. God loves us very much. He wants to speak and to have us listen. He also wants us to speak to Him and know *He* listens. He longs to be in relationship with us."

After a quiet pause to let this truth soak in I felt led to say, "This is the reason He sent Jesus."

With a puzzled look, he said, "Jesus?"

"Yes, you know, Jesus," I said. "Born at Christmas, died and rose again at Easter. Jesus."

Still puzzled, he responded, "What does Jesus have to do with God calling me?"

"Jesus is the bridge between God and man," I answered. "That's why God sent Him, so we could connect with God the Father through Him. He knew we couldn't make it on our own. We need help. That's why He sent Jesus to die for our sins or for our mistakes, like the ones you talked about a little while ago."

"Let me get this straight," he said. "God created me and wants to communicate with me, to have a relationship with me? And because He loves me and knew I'd make mistakes and muck up my life, He sent Jesus?"

"Yes, that's about the size of it," I replied.

As we were fast approaching London, I said, "Alvin, here is my card. I live in Guildford. My husband and I would be glad to talk to you and try to answer any questions you might have about all these things. Before we part, would you let my friend and me pray for you?"

"Sure," he replied, "why not?"

So standing on a train with our new friend, Denise and I gently touched his shoulder and prayed, "Dear God, thank You for Alvin, for creating him. Thank You that You know everything there is to know about him and that You love him. God, we know that You are calling him, communicating in ways that he can comprehend. Thank You for speaking to him. Help him to hear and understand. We ask that You reveal Your Son, Jesus, to him so he can know You better. Thank You for this opportunity of meeting each other today. Amen."

As we departed from the train and walked toward the taxi stand together, Alvin said, "I certainly wish I could take you two to lunch to thank you for your time, but I'm on my way to have tea with Princess Anne to discuss the 'Save the Children' benefit. Thanks for everything." As he shook our hands and proceeded to climb into a taxi and ride away with a wave, Denise and I looked at each other.

"Denise, did he say what I think he said?"

She nodded. "Let's go to a record store and see if anyone's ever heard of this guy."

We found a music shop, walked in and asked the sales clerk if he had ever heard of a singer named Alvin Stardust. "Certainly, ladies. Follow me." He led us to the pop section and pulled out an album with Alvin's picture on it. "This is his latest," the polite salesman said, "but I believe he has something new coming out at any time. Would you like to place an order for it?"

"Not at this time," I replied slowly. "Thank you."

After a few moments of silence, Denise expressed my very thought: You never know whom God is going to call you to pray for.

About a week later, my phone rang and Alvin Stardust spoke these words: "Nothing in my life has been the same since I met you two on the train. God sure is communicating with me! A few days after meeting you, Cliff Richard called me up and invited me to go to church with him." I listened with amazement. I knew that Cliff is a famous British pop star and a committed Christian.

"We went to Gerald Coates' church in Cobham, and at the end of his talk he asked if there was anyone who had never accepted Jesus. Gerald said, 'If there is anyone who wants to accept Jesus into his life, stand up.' I just stood up! I wonder if I might come around and talk to you and your husband about all the things going on in my life? I have a few questions."

This began a wonderful relationship with Alvin and his family. We spent many marvelous hours together discussing how God communicates with us and the importance of prayer. It was exciting to see all of the changes in his life and how it affected so many others. Another committed Christian and British pop singer, Sheila Walsh, invited Alvin to participate in some joint projects. (Sheila is also known for her work in the United States with The 700 Club.) Sheila Walsh, Gerald Coates and Cliff Richard all helped to disciple Alvin.

When Alvin answered the call to accept Jesus, he not only received salvation but also entered into a healed relationship with his Creator, a relationship in which he can communicate intimately about every aspect of his life.

This is the choice each one of us faces. Will we enter into relationship with God? Will we learn to communicate with Him through prayer? Our quest for wholeness begins here.

As we continue to explore this marvelous relationship available to us, let's remember with gratitude that Jesus' work on the cross laid the foundation so that His healing touch might reach every area of our lives.

TWO

THE MOST IMPORTANT TYPE OF HEALING

The most important and necessary part of a person's total healing is salvation—actually coming to know Jesus as one's personal Savior. In fact, salvation is the ultimate healing, for it is through salvation that we are able to share eternity with Jesus. In the Christian faith, salvation is the foundation upon which everything else builds.

Often people come forward in healing lines or ask others to pray for them for healing and they do not have a personal relationship with the Lord. All they know is that they have been diagnosed with cancer or been given six months to live with AIDS or some other debilitating illness. They are frightened and truly need the peace of knowing Jesus. For them to meet Christ brings tremendous healing, both physically and emotionally. When faced with a crisis, it is very comforting to know that you are not alone, that there is someone larger than this disease.

When I served as director of prayer ministry for Christian Healing Ministries in Jacksonville, Florida, a young man with

AIDS came to us desiring prayer for physical healing. As my prayer partner and I listened attentively to his story, it became obvious that he was truly searching for peace in his life, the peace that only Christ can give, the peace that passes all understanding (see Philippians 4:7).

Dr. Tom Wikstrom, a Christian psychiatrist, was my prayer partner on this particular day. Dr. Tom, as we call him, began kindly and gently to tell this young man about Jesus. He shared how he could know Jesus as a personal friend. When Dr. Tom had finished speaking, I said, "Would you like me to lead you through a little prayer? This would be a prayer inviting Jesus into your life."

"Yes, oh, yes!" he replied with tears in his eyes.

We bowed our heads and he prayed a simple prayer: "Dear God, thank You that You created me and love me. I've made mistakes, God, and I ask You to forgive me. Thank You for sending Jesus to die for my sins. I ask You, God, to come into my life and begin to reveal yourself to me through Your Son, Jesus. Thank You, God, for loving me so much. Amen."

When we finished praying, he looked at us with tears running down his face and said, "I have always wanted to do this, but I didn't know how. I've gone to a church that never really talked about Jesus or how to get connected to God. Thank you so much."

This young man died seven months later. God did not heal his physical illness, but He healed his spirit and his relationship with his Lord. This man received the ultimate healing: a restored, reunited relationship with his Creator.

Many people, like this young man, do not know how to "get connected" with God. They are thwarted in their personal journeys toward Jesus. There are many reasons, but one of the most tragic is the abuse they suffer along the way by well-meaning Christians. Enthusiastic believers sometimes forget that they must earn the right to speak to others about their faith by first showing unconditional love and no judgment. I think many of us have experienced the opposite of sensitivity, the person who says "Turn or burn, Sister!" Not at all what we could call loving, and certainly too abrupt to be effective.

My father-in-law, Father Frank Dearing, taught me many things about the importance of sensitivity in relationships with God's people. One of the questions he taught me to ask was, "How did you and the Lord get to know each other?" This is a beautiful lead-in for someone to share about his church affiliation, religious beliefs, years as a choirboy, or whatever.

And often we hear this response: "The Lord? I don't know. I don't even know that I know the Lord. I'm just sick (or going through a divorce or loss of job or another crisis). What does the Lord have to do with anything?"

Years ago, while living in England, I learned a metaphor that has helped me determine where people are spiritually. It even helps me determine where I am spiritually. It is just a little story. Jesus often spoke in parables, and I find that most of us, regardless of age, enjoy hearing them.

Imagine that as we drive along in the journey of life, we see Jesus on the side of the road. Most of us pick Him up and put Him in the trunk in case we get into trouble and need Him—just like a spare tire!

As we travel along, we come to a place where we decide to let Jesus come out of the trunk and sit in the backseat for a while. It feels a little safer knowing He is back there. We converse with Him and find that He seems genuinely interested in us. We also recognize that He is not a backseat driver; He does not try to take over the controls of the car.

Some of us enter a place in our spiritual journeys where we decide that it might be nice to invite Jesus to come up and sit in the front passenger seat. It feels good to have Him there. We enjoy being close to Him and spending more time with Him.

One day we ask Jesus, "Why is it I don't have peace in my life?"

He answers, "Because I'm not driving your car."

This is very frightening; we are not at all sure that we want Jesus to drive. We do not want to relinquish control of our lives to anyone, including Jesus. This is a trust issue.

Every single person knows where Jesus is sitting in the car of his or her life. Everyone reading this today knows where Jesus is. You know, too.

For instance, do you sometimes drive close to the places where you know He hangs out in hope of seeing Him?

Do you know where on the road you can find Him? Do you drive by often, looking at Him and longing to stop and invite Him into your car?

Have you picked Him up yet?

If He is in your car, are you happy with His location?

You know today, right now, where Jesus is sitting. In fact, why not make a note of it?

Today, _____ *(date), I have Jesus in the*

_____

position in the car of my life.

Is there another place you would like Him to be? Who can change that?

And consider: If Jesus is driving the car of your life, are *you* being a backseat driver?

Now, it may be that you have been starting to wonder about Jesus, or maybe you note readily that Jesus is not in your car. If so, I urge you to consider that He is speaking to you. Consider whether or not spiritual healing in your life, the healing that is only available through Christ, is what you truly want. If so, I hope and pray that you will read through the following two prayers. Decide which one is most suited to your heart and feelings. Then read it very slowly, concentrating and focusing on speaking the words to God. You may also add any additional prayers of your own. God knows your heart and He rejoices over your communication.

Lord Jesus, I need You. Thank You for dying on the cross for my sins. I open the door of my life and receive You as my Savior and Lord. Thank You for forgiving my sins and giving me eternal life. Take control of the throne of my life. Make me the kind of person You want me to be. Amen.

Or this:

My Lord Jesus, I have lived my life my way. I have done many wrong things. I repent of all my sin. Please forgive me. I trust You now to be my Savior. Thank You for dying in my place. I ask You now for Your gift of eternal life. I give my life to You and I want You to be my Lord. Help me live for You by the power of Your Holy Spirit. These things I pray in Jesus' name. Amen.

Assurance of Salvation

Have you accepted Jesus as your Lord and Savior? Do you still feel anxious about your salvation? You are not alone. Many people who have accepted Jesus into their hearts and who are practicing Christians still experience anxiety about their eternal salvation. They fear death because they might not have accomplished enough "good deeds" to ensure their acceptance by God. Again, this is because of our works-oriented society, in which we learn that we must earn our way.

I have prayed with many wonderful Christians through the years who feared death. They did not understand that they could know for certain that they would spend eternity with the Lord. In the Evangelism Explosion Program previously mentioned, we learned to ask two questions that help people understand God's desire for their peace and assurance.

The first question is: "If you die tonight, do you know for certain that you would go to heaven?" I have heard the full gamut of responses—everything from "I am absolutely positive" to "I know without a doubt that I would not go to heaven."

The second question receives interesting responses as well: "If you die tonight, and God meets you at the gate and says, 'Why should I let you into My Kingdom?' what would you say?" The answers are often similar to the ones given in the story of Saint Peter and the hundred points.

These questions open the way for us to explain what the Bible has to say about the eternal destiny of believers.

Many churches never teach about salvation and the assurance of salvation. As a result, many of their members do not know the promises mentioned in Scripture that could bring them much peace, verses such as 2 Peter 3:9, which says, "The Lord is not slow in keeping his promise, as some understand slowness. He is patient with you, not wanting anyone to perish, but everyone to come to repentance."

John 3:16 is one of the first Scriptures taught to Christians: "For God so loved the world that he gave his one and only Son, that whoever believes in him shall not perish but have eternal life." Another promise is found in John 6:47, which states, "I tell you the truth, he who believes has everlasting life." The Scripture that says it most clearly is 1 John 5:13: "I write these things to you who believe in the name of the Son of God so that *you may know that you have eternal life*" (emphasis added). God wants us to know that we have eternal life!

My English friend who trained us for the street ministry with Open Air Campaigners had a clever little comment about this very subject. He used to say that to be a Christian is "not just pie in the sky when you die, but steak on the plate while you wait!" The point is that God wants us to live an abundant life here on earth while we joyfully await going to heaven. We can live with wonderful peace and joy when we have this assurance.

While I was on staff at Christian Healing Ministries I worked in a number of areas to help people find healing physically, emotionally, mentally and spiritually, including praying with people, teaching and encouraging the prayer ministers.

A dear older woman contacted me at CHM about becoming involved in the healing ministry. Jean was always smiling and excited about everything that involved healing. She had read many books on the subject and loved coming to the ministry to receive prayer, to pray for others and to attend classes. In her church she was coordinator of the intercessors and also the catalyst behind developing healing teams. Jean had not accepted the call of Christ in her life until her senior years. She often regretted that she had not known Jesus years before when she was a social worker and a young mother. But when she accepted the call of Christ, she purposed in her heart to serve Him until the day she died, which she did faithfully for seven years.

When Jean became incapacitated with leukemia and unable to drive, she prayed for people over the telephone and organized the prayer chain for her church. During the last six months of her life, Jean and I talked a lot about the assurance of salvation and how the Lord was preparing a place for her on the other side. As a result of this knowledge, she died with great peace.

Jean had lived a very moral and productive life by the world's standards, but she, like Paul, would say that she counted it all as filthy rags compared to the glory she experienced in Christ Jesus.

Jean is an excellent example of two important dynamics in becoming a Christian servant. The first is that it is never too late to answer the call of Christ. The second is that through the Holy Spirit we can accomplish great things. But Jean's assurance of salvation did not come through all the wonderful work she had been able to do for the Lord. Rather, it came solely through the grace of God and her relationship with her Savior.

The Healing Power of the Holy Spirit

If we have grasped the powerful truth that we are saved by the blood of Jesus and bound for heaven, then we will want to share that truth with others. We are equipped for this work through the healing ministry of the Holy Spirit.

It is the Holy Spirit who first begins to reveal the Person of Jesus to us, and then it is this same Holy Spirit who empowers us to become stronger Christians, thus enabling us to lead others to Jesus' salvation.

To be effective in any ministry, especially the healing ministry, it is essential to draw on the power of the Holy Spirit. Although we see the hand of the Holy Spirit at work throughout the Old Testament—from the point of "hovering over the waters" in Genesis 1 to inspiring each of the prophets to speak for God—the promise of *our* access to the Holy Spirit only came as Jesus completed His mission on earth.

In the gospel of John, Jesus comforted His disciples while anticipating His own departure from this earth. He said that through the Holy Spirit they would do greater things than even He had done.

> "Believe me when I say that I am in the Father and the Father is in me; or at least believe on the evidence of the miracles themselves. I tell you the truth, anyone who has faith in me will do what I have been doing. He will do even greater things than these, because I am going to the Father. . . . If you love me, you will obey what I command. And I will ask the Father, and he will give you another Counselor to be with you forever—the Spirit of truth."
>
> JOHN 14:11–12, 15–17

After Jesus' ascension into heaven, the Holy Spirit was sent to empower all of us to complete the mission He began here. As recorded in the first chapter of Acts, the waiting disciples received the power of the Holy Spirit in an event that the Bible calls the baptism in (or *of*) the Holy Spirit. I want to explain a little about the release of this power of the Holy Spirit and talk about the name that we have given to this event. Christians most often use the term *baptism in the Holy Spirit* because that is the wording most Bible translations use when describing this event. We also might use the terms *release of the Holy Spirit* and *empowering by the Holy Spirit*. This concept appears in the book of Acts, in Paul's letters and even in Jesus' own anticipation of what was to come.

The Greek word is *baptizo*. This is a word used to describe what happens when a ship is totally submerged. Water flows over its decks, through its portholes, into the hull and nave. The ship is totally consumed by the water. In other words, it is "baptized." That word is wonderfully descriptive of what happens when the Holy Spirit is released in us to operate fully.

We distinguish baptism in the Holy Spirit from baptism with water for salvation because they are distinct events, occurring either at different times or at the same time. When we are baptized with water, that is, baptized for salvation into the body of believers, and we receive Jesus as Savior, the Holy Spirit comes to live in us. We become the temple of the Holy Spirit. This was Jesus' promise to us.

At that point, we can say that we know Jesus as Savior, because we have accepted Him as Savior. We depend on Him for our salvation, for our eternal life. But we may not at that point be able to say that we know Jesus as Lord. This is an important distinction. When we refer to Jesus as Lord and Savior, we are not being redundant; the words have separate meanings.

Knowing Jesus as Savior means that I am dependent on His death and resurrection for my salvation, for my eternal life with Him. To say that I know Jesus as Lord means that I am trying to live my life today according to the way He would have me live it. I accept the standard He has given for the conduct of my life. In other words, Jesus is driving my car.

Paul tells us in 1 Corinthians 12:3 that no one can honestly say Jesus is Lord except by the Holy Spirit. It is only because the Holy Spirit is living within us that we can hear and follow the Word of God and live a life pleasing and acceptable to Him.

37

The baptism in the Holy Spirit, on the other hand, occurs when the Holy Spirit, already residing in us from the time we accepted Jesus as Savior, is released to operate fully and completely in our lives. The question then is not, "Do we have the Holy Spirit?" but rather, "Does the Holy Spirit have us?" That is the distinction.

Water baptism, as an outward sign of the inner working of salvation, and baptism in the Holy Spirit seem for most people to occur at two separate times. In the life of Jesus, our example, baptism in the Holy Spirit occurred as a separate event.

Note that from day one of His conception, Jesus had the Holy Spirit. He was conceived by the Holy Spirit. There was never a moment in His life when He was not God, when He was not one with His Father and the Holy Spirit.

And yet, for the first thirty years of His life, no ministry by Jesus is recorded, other than that occasion when He was found in the Temple as a young boy listening and answering questions about the Father. There is no recorded teaching, and there are no recorded miracles, nothing—until He is baptized at the River Jordan at the hands of John the Baptist. "And as he was praying, heaven was opened and the Holy Spirit descended on him in bodily form like a dove" (Luke 3:21–22).

So, what happened to Him at the River Jordan? Although others were being baptized with water for salvation, this was unnecessary for Jesus. There was no sin in His life and He was already one with the Father. Nor could it be that He received the Holy Spirit then, because He already had the Holy Spirit in Him from His conception. Something else happened when the heavens opened and the Spirit descended on Him like a dove. It was an empowerment—a release of the Spirit's power—which has been described as baptism in the Holy Spirit.

This same baptism that Jesus received at age thirty—this release of the Spirit's power—is available to us so that we may be more like Jesus.

In the practice of the first-century Church, these two distinct baptisms frequently were combined into a single ceremony. The officiating minister would baptize with water for salvation and then, if one of the apostles was present, or someone designated by them to act on their behalf, the new Christians would receive the laying on of hands that they might receive the baptism in the Holy Spirit.

In Acts 8:12–17, we see an occasion when no one was present who could pray for the new converts to be baptized with the Holy Spirit. After the new believers accepted the faith and were baptized by Philip with water, Peter and John were dispatched from Jerusalem (a week's journey) to Samaria in order to lay hands on the new believers that they might be baptized with the Holy Spirit as well, "because the Holy Spirit had not yet come upon any of them; they had simply been baptized into the name of the Lord Jesus" (Acts 8:16).

As centuries passed, infant baptism became a common practice, especially in the sacramental churches, and, thus, the release of the Holy Spirit came at a later point. It was intended that this take place at confirmation when the young person made a public confession of faith, but somewhere along the line, bishops and confirmands lost sight of this purpose for confirmation, and it largely stopped happening. The baptism in the Holy Spirit—Pentecost—now most often occurs in small prayer groups where Holy Spirit–baptized believers lay hands on other believers and pray that they receive the release of the Spirit.

This new experience of God's power is available to all believers. When Peter addressed the crowd at Pentecost and the hearts of the people were moved, they asked him and the other apostles what they should do. Peter replied, "Repent and be baptized, every one of you, in the name of Jesus Christ for the forgiveness of your sins. And you will receive the gift of the Holy Spirit. The promise is for you and your children and for all who are far off—for all whom the Lord our God will call" (Acts 2:38–39).

The Army of God

Must everyone be baptized in the Holy Spirit? That is a question often asked. The short answer is no. The long answer is that, as we have seen, everyone *can* be baptized in the Holy Spirit. It is available to everyone, although it is not essential for salvation. My husband, Peter, uses an analogy that I believe explains this better than any I have ever heard.

In the Kingdom of God, there are citizens—all the people who have accepted Jesus as their Savior. The Kingdom of God also has an army. The army is made up of the people who are baptized in the Holy Spirit and who have the full power of the Holy Spirit released in them. This is a strictly volunteer army.

We enlist in this army when we ask for the baptism of the Holy Spirit. Once we have enlisted, we are taught how to use the weaponry of the Holy Spirit. These are the gifts of the Spirit, which are listed in 1 Corinthians.

> Now to each one the manifestation of the Spirit is given for the common good. To one there is given through the Spirit the message of wisdom, to another the message of knowledge by means of the same Spirit, to another faith by the same Spirit, to another gifts of healing by that one Spirit, to another miraculous powers, to another prophecy, to another distinguishing between spirits, to another speaking in different kinds of tongues, and to still another the interpretation of tongues. All these are the work of one and the same Spirit, and he gives them to each one, just as he determines.
>
> 1 CORINTHIANS 12:7–11

We are taught to use these weapons in ministering to the citizens of the Kingdom and to other members of the army of God. In addition, we are taught to use these gifts of the Holy Spirit for the protection of the citizens from the enemy and to retrieve lost souls from the enemy's territory.

We have to keep in mind that the other citizens of the Kingdom of God are not the enemy. There should never be strife among Christians such as we see in petty denominational rivalry or in deadly conflicts such as in Northern Ireland. That is a foreign concept to the Holy Spirit and not at all pleasing to God. I believe that this separation of Christians has taken place in the Church because of a lack of teaching on the subject.

My particular denomination witnessed certain people who were baptized in the Holy Spirit and then separated themselves from the rest of the church. They treated others as second-class citizens in the Kingdom. This has been to the shame of the Holy Spirit. It is not what He wants for us.

In fact, it is the work of the Holy Spirit to do just the opposite: The Holy Spirit works to unite. He united God and man at the incarnation of Jesus. He unites us together as Christians into one body, that is the Body of Christ. Things that separate us from one another are contrary to His will and work.

During the year my husband and I lived in England and developed evangelism teams, we found that the most powerful teams were the ones that were ecumenical; that is, they were composed of members of various Christian church denominations. When we accepted invitations to go into certain churches and teach about evangelism, street ministry and healing prayer teams, we found that the most powerful teams were those that incorporated people from many churches working together as a single unit. The Holy Spirit honored the ministry of these ecumenical teams by giving more power to their work. Remember, the manifestation of the Spirit is given *for the common good.*

This model allows each person to operate fully in his or her unique God-given talents, thus forming a complete Body. It is through working together that the Body of Christ can most effectively do the work of the Father. That really is the work of the Holy Spirit today. It is a unifying work. It is a work that brings us closer to God the Father, and to one another.

41

The Process of Holy Spirit Baptism

What happens to us after the baptism of the Holy Spirit? First we experience a time of celebration, a time of excitement, a time of exuberance. Generally the more extroverted a person, the more excited and exuberant is his reaction. Personally, I can honestly say that I was one of those who should have been locked up for at least six months and not allowed to overwhelm unsuspecting Christians or potential Christians. (My husband says perhaps a year.)

Some of the mistakes I made during this time cause me to cringe whenever I think of them. For instance, my friend Libby, who considered herself agnostic, followed me as president of the Junior Woman's Club of Jacksonville. One day, Libby called me on the phone to ask how I had developed a budget for my year as president.

My answer to her that day still makes me want to put my hand over my face and hide with embarrassment. I said, "Libby, the way I developed my budget was to sit down and pray and ask for the Lord's guidance. This would be the best place for you to start."

This did not help her in the least! The woman wanted to know on a practical level how to prepare a budget. I was not only no help, but I surely offended her in the process. The Lord was not glorified by this. The best witness would have been helping her with patience and technical assistance.

But I was irrepressible. If, during this time of exuberance, you had asked to borrow a nail file, I would probably have said something like, "Honey, you don't need a nail file. Jesus can file your nails."

Have any of you ever encountered this type of Christian? Have any of you ever been this type of Christian? I have asked forgiveness from God and from the people I could locate whom I am quite sure I offended. This experience has helped my commitment to the importance of good teaching on this subject.

Close on the heels of the time of celebration is a time of housecleaning. If you have received the baptism of the Holy Spirit, you know exactly what I mean. The Holy Spirit begins to reveal to us things in our lives that are not pleasing to God. I once heard a person say that before he was baptized in the Holy Spirit he drank a lot of alcohol. He drank as much as he wanted. After the baptism of the Holy Spirit, he still drank as much as he wanted; he just did not want to drink anymore! The Holy Spirit says, "You know this thing that you do? That's not such a good thing anymore." Thus, He takes away, in part, the desire to do things displeasing to the Lord. To the extent that the desire is taken away from us, He gives us the power to resist temptation.

Imagine a dry sponge. What happens to that dry sponge if it is put into a puddle of dirty water? It soaks up the dirty water, right? But take that same dry sponge and fill it with oil and then put it in that puddle of dirty water. You will find that it does not soak up the dirty water anymore. In fact, oil will spread out of the sponge until the entire puddle is covered with it.

That is much like what happens to us when we receive the empowerment of the Holy Spirit. Like sponges full of oil in a puddle of water, we can, as the Bible instructs us, live in the world and not be of the world. We can bring the truth of God's power to other people because we are no longer distracted by our own sinfulness. We are able to focus more on Jesus and let His love pour out to others. And just as the sponge must be constantly replenished with oil to have this effect, so we must continue being filled with the Holy Spirit.

The next thing the Holy Spirit does, which often happens simultaneously, is bring us into a more intimate relationship with Jesus. Because of Jesus, God's people no longer need a human high priest to enter the Holy of Holies and speak to Him on our behalf, as the Jews did in the Old Testament. We can now speak to Him directly and, more importantly, *hear* from Him directly through our Great High Priest, Jesus. While

43

this direct line of communication between us and God the Father is opened at the time of our salvation, we might say that the baptism of the Holy Spirit makes for clearer reception.

For instance, the Holy Spirit helps us to understand the Scriptures. We can read things in the Bible that we have read before the baptism of the Holy Spirit and discover entirely new concepts there. He opens up Scripture to us in a way that simply cannot be experienced until that event happens.

Another example of how the Holy Spirit brings us into closer relationship with Jesus has to do with Jesus' promise to guide us into all truth. Truth is not defined as scientific knowledge. Truth in the context of Scripture means that we have knowledge of the essence and the mind of God Almighty. This impartation is the work of the Holy Spirit.

The Holy Spirit also empowers us to move out in ministry. We first see this in the book of Acts when the disciples acted boldly for the faith. These verses are often quoted as the things that will happen to us as well when the Holy Spirit comes upon us. Again, this is a promise of Jesus. He says, "Do not leave Jerusalem, but wait for the gift my Father promised, which you have heard me speak about. For John baptized with water, but in a few days you will be baptized with the Holy Spirit" (Acts 1:4–5).

With these words, Jesus gave immediacy to His earlier promise that we would be empowered to do everything He did, and even greater things, after He returned to the Father and sent the Holy Spirit to be with us. These greater acts include performing miracles and healing God's wounded creation.

And one final example of the Holy Spirit at work in our relationship with Jesus is found in Jesus' last words to His disciples before He ascended into heaven. Since these were His last words, we might assume that He wanted them to be seen as very important words. He said: "But you will receive power when the Holy Spirit comes on you; and you will be my witnesses in Jerusalem, and in all Judea and Samaria, and to the ends of the earth" (Acts 1:8).

44

Once we operate in the power of the Holy Spirit, we become His witnesses. How do we witness to the world that the Kingdom of God is at hand—that God wants to restore the lost and hurting world to a perfect relationship with Him? The answer simply is that we do what Jesus did. We bring healing first and then proclaim the restoration of relationship. When God's people are in pain—physical pain, emotional pain, mental pain—they are not in a position to experience the love of God as He wants them to experience it. We must first deal with the pain, the disease, the mental anguish.

When people experience God's healing touch, they are then ready for whatever else He has for them. They are ready to begin to understand His love for them.

We are witnesses. We are witnesses to others of God's wondrous love for us through Jesus. We are by the power of the Holy Spirit able to work in unity and love with other Christians to do God's healing work here on earth.

Do you remember the song many of us used to sing about this kind of unity? "We are one in the Spirit; we are one in the Lord."

May the world know that we are Christians "by our love" for God and for each other.

THREE

THE FIRST BLOCK: OUR IMAGE OF GOD

> The LORD is gracious and compassionate, slow to anger and rich in love. The LORD is good to all; he has compassion on all he has made. . . . The LORD is faithful to all his promises and loving toward all he has made.
>
> PSALM 145:8–9, 13

Healing our image of God is one of the most basic and necessary healings of all. A distorted image of God stands in the way of approaching Him, making it all but impossible to want to receive His healing touch.

We human beings tend to create God in our own image, and this image is developed from a variety of experiences, places, situations and relationships. It may come from one's own earthly father who was not aware of his child's existence or perhaps deserted his family. It may come from having an abusive or critical father or paternal figure. Perhaps this distorted image resulted from one of God's representatives such as a priest, nun, pastor or teacher who was abusive or harshly critical. It may be that our Old Testament image of God is an angry and distant being, and we have never considered anything different.

Wherever a distorted image of God began, it is necessary to receive healing from the damage it caused. Until this healing takes place, the resulting anger or fear will continue to block a right relationship with God the Father.

After accepting Jesus and receiving the healing that comes from salvation, healing one's image of God is usually the beginning of the healing journey. It is a vital step that brings a person into intimacy with God and helps him or her to grow in the Christian faith.

Joyce, a friend from church, had great difficulty seeing God as loving or kind. She needed to receive deep healing from a memory of her childhood before she could change her view. Growing up, Joyce loved her dad immensely, deriving tremendous pleasure from just being with him. One beautiful autumn day, when Joyce was about twelve years old, they were working in the yard together raking leaves.

Joyce, full of joy and delight, turned to her father with outstretched arms and exclaimed, "Daddy, I just love you so much! I love you more than anybody else in the whole world!" Her father proceeded to take off his belt and beat her repeatedly. As he beat her, he yelled, "You are never to love anyone more than God! Never, never! Not me, not anyone! Do you understand me?"

This created enormous pain and confusion in Joyce's heart, confusion that would take many years to heal and restore. Today, Joyce realizes this incident was a result of her father's own distorted method of teaching his children about God, yet for years, it prevented her from believing that God could possibly be loving, merciful or tender.

How Our Pictures of God Become Distorted

We will look here at a few of the examples of abuse that cloud our views of God. In order to see God as loving and

48

benevolent, it is necessary to experience healing from these abusive experiences. Healing of abuse involves being cut free emotionally and spiritually from the person or persons who did the abusing. Generational healing may be necessary where a repeated pattern of abuse has been in the family. Inner healing from the memories of the abuse is also necessary. There may further be a need to pray through areas where drugs, alcohol or the occult were involved. These basic healing methods will be more clearly explained in chapters 5, 7 and 9.

Our Fathers as Primary Examples

In order to enjoy an intimate and loving relationship with God the Father, one must first deal with any areas that need healing in the relationship with one's earthly father.

God is referred to repeatedly in Scripture as "Father." Jesus called Him Father and told His disciples to do the same: "This, then, is how you should pray: '*Our Father in heaven,* hallowed be your name'" (Matthew 6:9, emphasis added).

When fathers are present, predictable, positive and loving, children tend to think of God as caring and of themselves as valuable. Children with absent fathers have likely not experienced that nurture and love.

In healing her relationship with God, another friend of mine, Edie, had to tell herself repeatedly that God was not like the person who abused her or the father who had not protected her. She searched the Scriptures and meditated on the personality of God. She studied some of the Hebrew names for God, such as *Jehovah-Jireh,* which means "The Lord Will Provide" and *Jehovah-Rapha,* meaning "The Lord Who Heals."

Could you trust your earthly father? Was he a father who lovingly encouraged you, or was he critical, demanding or abusive? Did he protect you from harm so that you always felt safe and protected? Or did he allow others to hurt you or perhaps hurt you himself either physically, emotionally or both?

Rob, a counselor friend of mine, struggled with a distorted view of God. When Rob was a young boy, he was not as large as the other children in his class because he was almost a year younger. This set him up to be picked on by the other school-children, especially the boys. In his neighborhood, most of the other boys were older, and therefore much larger than Rob.

One day, while playing with the other boys in the neighborhood, the community bully beat him up in front of everyone. Running home with the boys close on his heels, Rob's heart was pounding. He ran in the door with blood and tears streaming down his face and told his mom what had happened to him. His father overheard.

Instead of offering comfort and protection, Rob's father grabbed him by the collar and jerked him. Shaking him until his teeth rattled, he said, "Stop that crying, you little sissy! Be a man and get back out there and fight!" He then proceeded to throw Rob out the front door, where he was beaten up a second time.

Over a period of time, Rob was able to forgive his father for this and other similar instances. Through forgiveness and inner healing, Rob has been able to understand the true nature of God and to accept God's love and protection. Through his own healing prayer and a restored relationship with God, Rob also learned to see his earthly father with new eyes and a deeper understanding.

The Place of Father Figures

People who are considered spiritual leaders have tremendous power in the lives of others. We trust that they are God's representatives and that He will speak through them. We believe the things they preach and when they are in authority we are afraid to dispute or question their theology or their behavior.

Spiritual abuse occurs when someone uses a place of leadership to control or manipulate others into doing what he or she wants. Healing from emotional or spiritual abuse by a representative of a church may be a long process.

When my best friend, Ann, was selling her house, a young couple signed a contract and put down a binder. When the couple discussed this with their pastor, however, he informed them they should not buy a house outside the district of his church, and proceeded to tell them to renege on their contract. It just so happened that he had his real estate license and knew of a wonderful house within his district that would be perfect for them. He would serve as their real estate agent for personal profit.

This is spiritual and emotional abuse!

Spiritual abuse is not always so obvious. Quite often our perceptions of God come from preaching we have heard and the ways in which priests or ministers have spoken to or taught us. If we come from a denomination or church that preaches hellfire and damnation, we are likely to be afraid of God.

And we are also alienated from God when a spiritual leader disappoints us by indulging in ungodly behavior. When churches have ministers or leaders who fall into traps of greed, sexual immorality or other sins, it can take years for people to recover. Many not only leave the church but totally separate themselves from any further relationship with God.

What were the messages you received about God? Was He portrayed as a loving God, or was He someone with a large stick waiting for you to mess up? Is He someone who is approachable, or do you view Him as frightening and distant?

Sexual Abuse by One in Authority

As powerful as spiritual and emotional abuse are in distorting a person's image of God, there is another even more damaging form of abuse. This is the area of sexual abuse.

Sexual abuse by a parental figure or trusted spiritual leader is devastating. Children particularly suffer serious ramifications because parents and leaders are truly viewed as God's

51

representatives. Being sexually abused or exploited is confusing and hurtful enough. But when the abuse comes from a trusted spiritual teacher or parent, a distortion of God is inevitable.

A very serious example of this occurred right here in Jacksonville. It was discovered that a youth pastor was having sex with several of the girls in his youth group. His father was the head pastor of the church and evidently was aware that there was cause for concern in this area. It was only after a worried mother of one of the girls read her diary that it was brought out into the open. Though both the pastor and the youth pastor resigned, the entire church was totally devastated.

Viewing God as the Cause of Pain

Another distorted image of God comes from believing that He has caused trauma or suffering. Most of us as children probably asked a special prayer that was not answered to our satisfaction. Perhaps a best friend was not healed or a loved one or a dear pet died.

Family members often make the well-meaning mistake of telling children something like this: "God loved your daddy so much that He took him to heaven to live with Him." What is the message here? God shows His love by killing people. How can we feel oneness with a God who takes away the people we love?

Let me mention that a much better explanation is that *death* took the loved ones from this earth. And God rescues us from death to live again forever with Him in heaven.

There will likely be times in our lives where we really believe that God has let us down or expected too much from us. The natural reaction to this is to be angry with God. Some Christians think it is great sin to express anger toward God, but this is not the case. God knows our feelings and respects our honesty. Consider how gently He dealt with both Moses and Jonah when they lashed out in anger at Him (see Numbers 11:11–23; Jonah 4:1–11).

Do you believe people can actually be angry with God? I do. And I believe that until we have forgiven God for those places where we feel He has let us down, we will not have intimacy with Him.

Now, you may be thinking, *Wait a minute! Did she just say that we could get mad at God? And did she really say that we might have to forgive God?*

Yes, I did say that. You were reading correctly. Note: I am *not* saying that God has made a mistake; *God is perfect.* Nor am I saying that God needs to be forgiven. Our anger with God is our problem, not His.

I am saying that in our broken human condition, we do not understand all of God's ways. As the book of Isaiah states: "'For my thoughts are not your thoughts, neither are your ways my ways,' declares the LORD. 'As the heavens are higher than the earth, so are my ways higher than your ways and my thoughts than your thoughts'" (55:8–9).

Whatever has caused us to be angry with God or disappointed by His perceived action or inaction stops us from going to Him in search of healing. Who would ask a favor of a king who was perceived to be intolerant, unloving or without understanding? If we have such a perception of God, and if this stops us from approaching Him with our needs, that perception must be healed before any other healing takes place. As we express forgiveness, the block of our anger is broken.

I learned this lesson when the Lord brought someone to me for ministry whose entire attitude toward God was one of bitterness, resentment and disillusionment. Larry came for ministry with me in the final stages of a terminal illness that had left him permanently blind.

Larry had been a church organist for many years and had felt close to God at various times in his life. Now, during our ministry sessions, he continually lashed out: "How could God have let this happen to me?"

53

One day he began ranting and raving, cursing God for his illness, for his blindness. He was screaming: "God isn't a God of love! God doesn't love me or this wouldn't have happened to me! I hate God! I don't want to have a thing to do with Him! I hate God!"

This went on for what seemed like forever, and I have to say it scared me. I had never seen anyone that angry with God before. During his verbal rampage I began to wonder if a person could be this angry with God and live to tell about it. I would not have been surprised if lightning bolts had come through my office window and struck us all.

After he finally calmed down, I suggested that we take a short break. I asked Mary, who was teaming with me, to get Larry some water while I went to the ladies' room. I went downstairs and locked myself in one of the stalls and tried to calm down. After a few minutes, I prayed: "God, I've never seen anyone this angry before. Larry is so angry with You. I don't know what to do."

Immediately, God spoke to me. He said: *Norma, it's okay. I know how angry Larry is with Me. I am still God. I am still going to be God. I am not going to fall off My throne because Larry is mad at Me. This is what I want you to do. I want you to go back upstairs and ask Larry if he can forgive Me for those places where he believes I have let him down.*

Feeling much calmer, I proceeded upstairs and asked Larry if he could forgive God for those places where he felt God had let him down. He quietly said, "I can try."

So we began to pray prayers of forgiveness, following a format that I will explain in the next chapter. With hands cupped together, Larry began to name everything he could think of and place it symbolically in his hands. He listed every situation in which he believed God had let him down.

As Larry began speaking from the depths of his heart, his feelings of deep sorrow, grief, despair and loneliness poured forth. The uncertainty of his illness, fear of the future and the question of who would take care of him loomed ominously.

54

He poured out to God the main reason for his intense anger: feeling abandoned by Him as well as others.

As these words rolled out of Larry's mouth, the peace of God began entering my office. The more Larry spoke, the more peace came until it felt as though waves of peace were flowing into the room and bathing over us. When Larry had put everything he could think of on the "pile" in his hands and we turned all of it over to God, we just sat in that beautiful and glorious peace.

Everything turned for Larry and his relationship with God that day. He was able to pray, listen to Christian tapes and praise God once again. He and God moved into a beautiful new intimacy they had never experienced before. Larry continued growing in his faith, making peace with his entire family and attending church regularly.

Remember the scene from the touching movie *Forrest Gump* with Lieutenant Dan at the top of the ship, hanging onto the mast during that ferocious storm? Swaying in the wind, with lightning and thunder crashing all around him, he screamed out his anger with God over losing his legs in Vietnam. He bellowed, "All right, God, let's have this out!" and he fussed and cussed and shook his fists at God.

After this, things began to turn for him. Their fishing boat was one of the few saved, their business increased and he was finally able to thank Forrest for saving his life. Forrest said it well: "I think Lieutenant Dan and God made their peace that day."

God is on the side of peace and love and life. In order to enter into intimate relationship with Him, we must let go of our anger, express forgiveness and seek Him for who He is, not whom we create Him in our limited understanding to be.

The True Picture

As you can see, we have the opportunity to develop many distorted images of God. How do we find the true picture? If

55

we want to know what God is really like, we look at Jesus. Because Jesus is God, He is the exact representation and image of God the Father.

> The Son is the radiance of God's glory and the exact representation of his being, sustaining all things by his powerful word. After he had provided purification for sins, he sat down at the right hand of the Majesty in heaven.
>
> HEBREWS 1:3

Jesus is the human face of God, His glorious visual aid!

And what do we see when we look at Jesus? We see how He was filled with compassion every time He encountered sickness and suffering. We see how He responded to hurt with action—healing the sick, casting out demons and preaching the Good News of the Kingdom.

Thus we see a new aspect of God's tremendous love. Not only did He send His Son to die in our places, so that we might live with Him forever, but He sent His Son to show us what He is like.

The closer we become to Jesus, the more intimacy we will have with God the Father. Remember Jesus' words to Philip: "Anyone who has seen me has seen the Father" (John 14:9). So we continue to look to the Person of Jesus to see what God is really like, allowing His words and His actions to be our guide.

Jesus seemed to love to talk about the Father's love and how He seeks us out. This was the subject of many of His parables. Luke 15:3–7 tells of the shepherd who leaves his flock to search diligently for one lost sheep. Likewise, the Good Shepherd cares deeply for the lonely, the outcast and the lost. In the parable about the Prodigal Son, told in Luke 15:11–31, Jesus described how a young man strayed and squandered his inheritance on lustful living. Yet, when he returned home in complete humiliation and with a repentant heart, his father rejoiced over his return and restored him to his full stature as a son.

Paul teaches in Romans that we can go to our "Abba," which is Hebrew for "Daddy," for all of our needs.

> For you did not receive a spirit that makes you a slave again to fear, but you received the Spirit of sonship. And by him we cry, "Abba, Father." The Spirit himself testifies with our spirit that we are God's children. Now if we are children, then we are heirs—heirs of God and co-heirs with Christ, if indeed we share in his sufferings in order that we may also share in his glory.
>
> ROMANS 8:15–17

Imagine! We can actually approach God as our Father and call Him something as intimate as Daddy!

In drawing closer to the Lord Jesus and receiving the necessary healing of our image of God, we begin seeing our Daddy God as loving and approachable. We begin to believe that yes, indeed, He "is gracious and compassionate, slow to anger and rich in love" (Psalm 145:8).

God loves us! Is that not great news? And not only does He love us, but He makes this promise: "Never will I leave you; never will I forsake you" (Hebrews 13:5). That is even better news. We will never call God and get an answering machine!

You want to hear what I believe is the best news yet? No matter where we go or what we do, we can never be separated from God's love. When I think of this, I believe it is the most awesome truth imaginable. *Nothing can ever separate me from the love of God.* Do you know what else this means? Nothing can ever separate you from the love of God, either.

> No, in all these things we are more than conquerors through him who loved us. For I am convinced that neither death nor life, neither angels nor demons, neither the present nor the future, nor any powers, neither height nor depth, nor anything else in all creation, will be able to separate us from the love of God that is in Christ Jesus our Lord.
>
> ROMANS 8:37–39

57

FOUR

THE SECOND BLOCK: SIN AND SEPARATION

After realizing who God truly is, what is it that prevents us from communicating with Him? What blocks us from talking to Him or listening to what He wants to say to us? The first and foremost thing, I believe, is our own sinfulness. The second is the guilt and shame we feel because of this sinfulness.

Sin is always a barrier that separates us from approaching God or feeling connected to Him. This is why He tells us over and over in Scripture to bring our sins before Him so we can be cleansed. "If we confess our sins, he is faithful and just and will forgive us our sins and purify us from all unrighteousness" (1 John 1:9).

Not only does God forgive us our sins, but He forgets them as well. Jeremiah says that He remembers our sins "no more" (Jeremiah 31:34).

At a concert once, I heard Christian evangelist Mike Warnke put it this way. He said, "Hey, God, You remember that sin I confessed a moment ago? And God's response was, 'No!'"

My husband, Peter, had a powerful experience with God along these lines some years ago when he attended Cursillo, a spiritual retreat. One night while Peter was lying in his bunk, God began to speak to him about his life and how He wanted them to become closer. Intimacy is always something God longs to develop.

Peter felt a certain alienation from God because of his sinfulness, but still God spoke to his heart. He said that He longed to be closer to Peter and for that to happen, they needed to get some things out of the way. In a mental picture God showed Peter a chalkboard and "placed" a piece of chalk in his hand.

Peter felt that God was saying, *Write your sins upon this chalkboard, and I'll leave them on the board for as long as it takes Me to forgive and forget them.* Peter did not want to start with anything too enormous, so he began by writing a few minor infractions.

As soon as he had finished putting those words on the board, he saw a hand with an eraser come along and erase them. Then he started writing more of his sins on the board, and the same eraser came along and wiped those away, too. Peter said that as fast as he wrote, the eraser followed behind the words. He found it amazing that the eraser seemed to move at exactly the same speed regardless of the degree of sin. This exercise continued for over an hour, then he felt cleansed and purified.

> Repent, then, and turn to God, so that your sins may be wiped out, that times of refreshing may come from the Lord, and that he may send the Christ, who has been appointed for you—even Jesus.
>
> ACTS 3:19–20

As Peter experienced God's forgiveness, his relationship with the Lord was renewed. He knew that as the sins were erased from the board they were forgotten by God, never to be remembered again. He realized that Satan might try to remind him of those sins later on, but he also knew that they no longer held him in bondage because the Lord had forgiven them and then forgotten them.

How Satan Keeps a Grip

Like Peter, we can count on the fact that Satan, the enemy, will do everything within his power to keep us in sin and bondage. Generally he uses two specific tools to remind us of our sins.

These are shame and guilt. I do not mean here the sense of conviction that we get from the Holy Spirit when we have disobeyed God, but an unrelenting self-torture about sins that the Lord will readily forgive. Satan's hope is that we will feel so bad about ourselves that we will be embarrassed to call on the Lord for forgiveness. He tries to convince us that God is alienated from us and could never accept us because our sin is so great.

There is one area I want to use as an example of this trap, because it is one in which Satan seems almost always to succeed. For many years I have witnessed consistent and unyielding self-accusation, the feeling of being too unworthy to receive forgiveness, in women coming for ministry who have one experience in common.

The outlying cause for prayer is healing of infertility. The woman is usually happily married and ready to begin having children. There are no medical or biological reasons for her to have difficulty conceiving.

Nevertheless, as her shame and alienation emerge, we find so often that there is a history of one or more abortions in her background that have yet to be resolved. When a woman, and many times a man, participates in an abortion, she tends to bury the event and move on with life. It is generally not until she is ready to have children that it resurfaces.

The words of shame and self-hatred almost seem to make infertility a self-fulfilling prophecy. Fear gets involved as well.

61

The unspoken thoughts are always the same: *God isn't going to bless me with a baby because of what I did* or *If He does bless me with a baby, it probably will not be a healthy baby because I'll be punished.*

When the abortion experience is brought before the Lord and a cleansing of guilt and shame takes place, a great weight is lifted—and the enemy's inner taunts are silenced. Many times—for this and other deeply felt issues that need to be brought to the Lord—it is accomplished not only through repentance but also through inner healing, a concept that we will discuss later.

The Lord often reveals Himself through prayer and brings a peace between the mother and child who was aborted. This is one of the most powerful and anointed healings I have ever witnessed.

It is always wonderful to receive that call from a woman who has received prayer for healing and who now says, "Guess what! We are expecting!" God truly wants us to bring shame and guilt out into the light and allow His healing power to forgive and cleanse.

Anyone who has experienced this kind of forgiveness—no matter what the sin—no longer fears being in God's presence. He or she is ready to be in communion with the Lord again.

Although we may think to the contrary, God never leaves us. We are the ones who stray. I remember once saying to the Lord, "I don't feel as close to You as I once did." He responded, *Well, who moved?* This helped me to realize that I had moved away. It was I who had changed the intimacy of my prayer life.

I want to mention another area of sinfulness resulting in deep shame and guilt because it is so prevalent. This is sexual misbehavior. Sexual misconduct includes sexual promiscuity, sex outside of marriage, adultery, homosexuality, pornography and sexual abuse.

When a person falls into this type of sinfulness, self-reproach will discourage him from going to church, spending time with other Christians or time with the Lord. A vicious cycle emerges beginning with sin, then withdrawal from God and others, and finally a deeper entry into the sin. The person begins to have a sense of hopelessness and helplessness.

A young Christian woman named Elizabeth came to see me once with problems in her marriage. It seemed that after approximately five years of marriage her husband, Simon, had left her, declaring he was gay and moving in with another man. She still loved him, felt a commitment to her marriage and was communicating with him regularly.

She also informed me that Simon had been sexually abused by his grandfather for years but had not remembered any of it until after his grandfather's recent death. He had also experienced a long struggle with alcoholism, which ran in the family, and had attempted to take his own life.

Elizabeth and I prayed diligently for Simon, as did her family and her church. I was able to explain to her some of the long-term effects of sexual abuse and the confusion that often sets in. I also shared about the shame and guilt that can grow like a cancer within us, and how the Lord is able to heal these places through forgiveness and inner healing.

The next week she called and said that Simon had moved back home and that she had shared some of our discussion with him. He wanted to know if I would meet with him and his wife and help them sort out all of these difficult issues. We agreed to meet the next week.

As this attractive couple came in and sat on my sofa, they were visibly nervous. Holding hands, we prayed for the Lord to give us peace, wisdom and direction. This is the story that began to unfold.

Simon was raised in an alcoholic home. He could never remember a time when he did not see his father with a cigarette in his mouth and a beer in his hand. The house was always in a state of upheaval, as his parents often had drunken brawls. He could never bring anyone home from school because his parents might be fighting or his father might be passed out on the floor.

He remembered one particular time when his parents had been drinking and had broken everything in the house. They had sent seven-year-old Simon to his room during this brawl. After hours of ranting, raging and finally sobering up, they sat down on the front steps and discussed burning the house down.

Simon was in his room with the window open and heard this conversation. He was terrified as he wondered if his parents would get him out before burning the house down or if his body would catch fire and burn.

As a result of his home situation, Simon spent a great deal of time with his grandparents. His grandmother loved him very much, but she really wished he had been a girl. She often dressed him as a girl with frilly dresses and bonnets and encouraged him to play with dolls. His grandfather regularly took him out to the shed in the backyard and sexually molested him.

Simon began to struggle with homosexual thoughts and feelings while he was in high school. It was also in high school that he met his wife. He was overjoyed to have found a best friend whom he also loved and desired. Simon and Elizabeth always had a loving and sharing relationship.

Simon shared with Elizabeth that he often struggled with depression and suicidal thoughts, but they both assumed it was a result of the alcoholic home. After they were married and he was in the military, Simon began drinking more and more. It was during one of these depressive episodes that he attempted to take his life.

Before his grandfather died, Simon visited him regularly in the hospital. Simon felt enormous conflict during these visits because at times he found that he actually enjoyed seeing his grandfather suffering and in pain. Shortly after his death, Simon began remembering the abuse.

This threw him into further confusion about his sexuality, and all of the homosexual thoughts and feelings he had previously experienced began to resurface. Satan began to whisper his lies: "You liked being with your grandfather. You're really gay." Simon began to worry that if anyone found out about the abuse they would blame him.

This put him into a downward spiral. He alienated himself from Elizabeth and church and God. He began going to gay bars and looking at pornography. He eventually believed the lies, moved in with a lover and tried to forget both Elizabeth and God.

What finally brought him to seek help was the fact that the gay lifestyle was emptier than anything else he had ever experienced. He realized that he still felt lonely and he really missed Elizabeth, who was the only person who had ever loved him unconditionally.

As the three of us prayed together, the Lord began to heal that little boy of his shame and guilt and fears. The Lord began to help Simon see himself as He saw him, a precious child who was a victim in a sick and broken world. Simon experienced hours of inner healing during which Jesus brought healing and restoration to those memories of his childhood.

Tremendous healing took place in the family as well, as Simon's grandmother also came for prayer and was able to apologize for not being aware of what was happening to him. She was able to take responsibility for her part. This brought Simon more healing.

Another one of the wonderful things that happened during this time was that Simon's father accepted the Lord and was healed of alcoholism. He gave his testimony at his church. Simon witnessed his father giving thanks to God for his healing and apologizing for the pain he had caused his family.

Simon and his father now have a new relationship in which they are able to share the love of Jesus. The last I heard from Simon and Elizabeth, they were active in their church and had been involved with foreign missions. Even though Simon still has to work at his recovery, he is no longer totally bound by shame or guilt or sin. His relationships with his family members *and* his relationship with God have been restored.

65

Sin is like the static you experience on a CB or a ham radio. It prevents us from hearing clearly or being able to communicate effectively.

The way to clear up the static and open the channel is with repentance and forgiveness. Only in this way will your relationship with God be healed. After this healing takes place, a desire and a yearning grows in your heart for healing and reconciliation in other relationships.

Where to Begin

If you know that sin—of whatever extent or whatever degree; sin is sin to God—is blocking you from communion with Jesus, let Him set you free.

The best way to begin is with an in-depth period of repentance, similar to what both Peter and Simon experienced. This can be accomplished in a number of ways. One way is to start chronologically by age and look at the areas where you feel you need to forgive or be forgiven. You might start by remembering preschool and continuing with elementary school, junior and senior high, etc. In prayer, ask the Lord to help you remember those areas that need healing and forgiveness. This is always something He loves to do, and with love and gentleness He will bring these areas to mind.

Forgiveness of people who caused wounding—parents, spouses, ministers, authority figures, those who should have been worthy of trust—is essential. Forgiveness is facing resentments and then facing the cross of Christ. If you bury the hurts, you bury the hates. If you bury the hurts and the hates, you bury the possibility of healing. When we hold unforgiveness or bitterness in our hearts, the end result usually hurts us more than anyone else.

This was the case with a Christian woman named Sandra who came for prayer about her problem with anger. As an elected official, Sandra was continually having altercations with other board members. She was becoming concerned about re-election.

It quickly became obvious that Sandra still had deep-seated hatred and resentment toward her previous husband, although they had been divorced for many years. This hatred had intensified when he married Sandra's best friend.

Because Sandra discussed her ex-husband through gritted teeth, making comments about running him over with her truck, it did not appear that she was coming for prayer about forgiveness of her previous husband or best friend. For this reason, we spent many prayer sessions praying about her childhood and other intimate relationships.

Trying to gain power and control of her life, Sandra had become interested in various types of occult involvement, opening dangerous spiritual doors. After renouncing her occult involvement (see chapter 9) and praying for deep inner and physical healing, Sandra began to experience a new oneness with the Lord Jesus.

After also experiencing the fullness of the power of the Holy Spirit, Sandra came in one day, sat down on my couch and said: "You think my spiritual and physical life would be even better if I would forgive my ex-husband, don't you?"

"Sandra," I replied, "whom does your hatred and bitterness hurt the most?"

After staring into my eyes for a long moment, Sandra said, "M-me and my children and grandchildren."

"That's true," I replied. "With the help of Jesus, Sandra, are you ready to give it up?"

"With the help of Jesus," Sandra replied, "I'll try."

That day, Sandra began making "stacks" of the things she needed to forgive and let go of, as I will explain shortly in the Four-Way Forgiveness exercise. As she turned over her hands, symbolically releasing the years of pain, sorrow, anger and grief, Sandra was transformed before my very eyes. By the power of the Holy Spirit, the hatred and bitterness that had consumed her for more than a decade were lifted from her heart and mind. Sandra became transformed by the miracle of supernatural grace.

Several months later, Sandra came to see me and was elated to share a story. She had seen her ex-husband across the gymnasium at her granddaughter's gymnastics meet. She said, "Norma, I looked across the gym, saw my ex-husband with his wife, and realized for the first time in years that I no longer hated them." She proceeded to tell me that to the surprise of her children and grandchildren she actually walked across the gym and cordially spoke to her ex-husband and his wife.

This is the healing grace of forgiveness—both the forgiveness we receive and the forgiveness we extend to others. Forgiveness is always available to those who reach out and accept it. By ourselves, it is impossible to forgive those who hurt us or to receive forgiveness. We need the supernatural grace only possible through the sacrifice of the cross.

There are many different ways to pray for repentance and forgiveness. Some people like to do this in two categories, sins of commission and sins of omission. Here are two possible ways. Ask the Lord what is right for you.

One method of forgiveness is to write sins you have committed on one piece of paper and sins committed against you on another. Then give these lists to the Lord by presenting them at the altar of your church, if you like, or perhaps burning the paper.

A second method called Four-Way Forgiveness is a procedure my father-in-law developed and I have used for many years. It has been beneficial for me personally and for others in the healing of unforgiveness and bitterness.

I encourage you to try this or perhaps another prayer that works for you as you address those sins for which you need forgiveness and those people whom you need to forgive.

The method or procedure of how you do this is not so important. The most important thing is that you repent of not forgiving others and that you receive God's forgiveness for this and other sins in your own life. Think of yourself as a drainpipe with clogs. The clogs are sin. Forgiveness of yourself and others allows the clogs to be washed away and healing water to run freely. This opens up the lines of communication between you and God.

The Four-Way Forgiveness Prayer

Part 1: Hold up to the Lord all the things about the person that trouble you.

Bring before the Lord all the things a particular person has done that bother you. Physically put your hands together and pile up, in your hands, all these things to give to Him. For example, if the person is your father, list and name those things that upset you about him. It is important to verbalize each offense as you place it in your hands. When you are finished, turn your hands over and release all of these things to the Lord. At this point, pray a prayer similar to the following:

Lord Jesus, I give You each one of these things and ask that You take them and pour Your love and healing power through them. I thank You, Lord, that You have the power and the grace to redeem them. I ask You, Lord Jesus, to lift all the pain and hurt that have been involved with each one of these experiences, that You lift it from my heart, from my mind, from my spirit. I ask that You lift the burden of these things from my shoulders. I give all this to You, Lord, and I trust You to deal with it. Thank You, Lord, for taking each one of these things. Amen.

Part 2: Hold up to the Lord all the things about you that trouble this person.

Put your hands together again and prepare to lift up all those things about yourself that may trouble the person you are forgiving. Then, go through the same process of verbally listing them and piling them up one by one in your hands. When you cannot think of anything else, turn your hands over and release those things to the Lord. Now, pray the same type of prayer:

Lord Jesus, I ask You to pour Your love and healing power over these things. I ask You to heal this hurt and pain and disappointment. Lord, I give You this relationship today and ask for You to deal with it. Help me to trust You with it. Amen.

Part 3: Hold up to the Lord your heart's desire for this person.

Hold out your hands as if to offer that particular person to the Lord and share with the Lord what the desire of your heart is for him or her. Say, "Lord, this is my dad and this is what I would like for You to do for my dad." (If the person has died, it is still okay to lift up the person in prayer and share with the Lord what the desire of your heart is for him or her.) List those things, placing them in your hands. When you are finished, turn your hands over and give them all to the Lord, just as before. At this point, pray a prayer like the following:

Lord, I give [name] to You. I thank You that You are able to handle [him/her] better than anyone else. Bring about Your perfect will for [name], and let Your love pour into [him/her] and Your healing power flow over [him/her]. I release [name] into Your care. Amen.

Part 4: Hold up to the Lord your heart's desire for yourself.

Lastly, hold yourself up to the Lord and share with Him what the desires of your heart are for yourself, what you would really like to see Jesus do in your life today. Name these things out loud, put them into your hands and release them.

Lord, I release these things to You and ask that You pour Your love, mercy and grace into them. I thank You that I can trust You with these things. Surround me with Your heavenly angels. Help me to know how much You love me. Continue to reveal Yourself to me in a mighty way. Thank You, Lord. Amen.

PART TWO

PRACTICAL
TOOLS FOR
HEALING

FIVE

GENERATIONAL HEALING

In the preceding chapters, we talked about how God wants to have a personal relationship with each of us. We also looked at what can block us from being able to "live and move and have our being" (Acts 17:28) in this relationship. In the next few chapters, we will address various healing tools that will help you move into this new and more complete relationship. The first of these tools is generational healing.

It is fairly easy to grasp the idea of genetic predisposition toward sickness. This is a purely human approach to understanding why people have certain illnesses and usually becomes apparent when filling out medical forms in a doctor's office or reading the newspaper or watching a program about genetics. We recognize that certain illnesses like cancer, arthritis and sickle cell anemia can have a genetic component. But what many people do not realize is that other generational influences exist. These can be even more debilitating, for they affect us not only physically but also spiritually, mentally and emotionally.

Scripture shows that all of us have been affected both positively and negatively by what has gone on in past generations. We know, for instance, that we are still affected by the sin committed by Adam and Eve in the Garden of Eden. In addition, we also see that the behavior and attitudes our ancestors had toward God still touch us today.

And he passed in front of Moses, proclaiming, "The LORD, the LORD, the compassionate and gracious God, slow to anger, abounding in love and faithfulness, maintaining love to thousands, and forgiving wickedness, rebellion and sin. Yet he does not leave the guilty unpunished; he punishes the children and their children for the sin of the fathers to the third and fourth generation."

EXODUS 34:6–7

At first glance these verses from Exodus might give us cause for concern, but we need only look at the following verses in Ezekiel to understand the full message:

"What do you people mean by quoting this proverb about the land of Israel: 'The fathers eat sour grapes, and the children's teeth are set on edge'? As surely as I live, declares the Sovereign LORD, you will no longer quote this proverb in Israel. For every living soul belongs to me, the father as well as the son—both alike belong to me. The soul who sins is the one who will die."

EZEKIEL 18:2–4

These two Scriptures may seem contradictory, but I believe they represent what my friend Edie calls "balancing truths." The one who sins has consequences and the one who is upright has consequences, implying a choice. If a woman is born into a family where the last ten generations of women have been alcoholics, she need not say, "I have no choice in this. I am doomed to become an alcoholic." She can make a conscious choice to pray to break the cycle of alcoholism through generational healing, by becoming involved in a group like Adult Children of Alcoholic Parents, and by realizing the potential danger of a susceptibility to alcohol.

Blessings as well as curses can be passed along from generation to generation. When Moses handed the Israelites the Ten Commandments, he also gave insight into generational effects:

76

"You shall not bow down to [idols] or worship them; for I, the LORD your God, am a jealous God, punishing the children for the sin of the fathers to the third and fourth generation of those who hate me, but showing love to a thousand generations of those who love me and keep my commandments."

DEUTERONOMY 5:9–10

This potential to affect "a thousand generations" with curses or blessings really came alive to me when a young man named Steve, a new Christian, came for prayer. Steve was from a very long line of Hindus. Everyone on both his mother's and father's sides of the family had practiced Hinduism for hundreds of generations.

Generational healing was so important to Steve that he actually moved to a different city where he knew he could receive ministry and become involved in Christian community. It was wonderful to consider that since Steve had chosen to love God and keep His commandments, he was not only receiving healing for himself but initiating God's love for a thousand generations to come after him.

It is often startling to realize the extent to which we are affected by our ancestors. Nevertheless, until we recognize that the circumstances of their lives can block the flow of the Holy Spirit in our lives, we will be prevented from walking in wholeness. These patterns have lasting effects in a family line until healing and repentance take place and break the influences.

Francis and Judith MacNutt, founders of Christian Healing Ministries, once prayed with a family that seemed to carry a predisposition to suicide. A couple came for prayer for their eight-year-old son, who kept pointing an imaginary gun to his head and pretending to pull the trigger. He also kept beating his head against the wall and talking about "ending it all."

A review of the family's history revealed that the mother's father and her maternal uncle had both committed suicide with a gun. The father's uncle also had committed suicide.

After prayer to break any genetic or spiritual predisposition to suicide, the boy no longer hit his head or spoke of death.

Coincidence? I do not think so—at least, not in my experience. It is as though a stronghold in the spiritual realm is broken when we pray and bring these destructive generational patterns before God.

How Patterns Begin

It is not always possible to trace a generational predisposition to its root. Generally, though, it begins in one of several areas. Here are four main root causes.

Habitual Sin

There is no question that sin operates as a destructive force in our lives. Sin also can have lasting consequences for our families. All sin begins as a thought and then proceeds to an action. When the action is repeated over a period of time, the sin becomes easier to commit and can further evolve into a habit.

Habitual sin, then, is an area in which someone continues to struggle over and over again. Habitual sin involves a loss of control, almost like a compulsion. We see examples of this in pornography, adultery, embezzlement and drug addiction. The enemy can get a foothold, or a power over our lives, when we engage in sin repeatedly, and especially when we are under the influence of drugs or alcohol. It becomes a vicious cycle.

Mark, a committed Christian missionary, opened a dangerous door to sin and destruction by sampling the drug cocaine. Then he used it again and again. The more he used it, the stronger the addiction became until finally he was stealing from his own church and family and lying about it in order to support his habit. He was arrested for robbing a store and spent time in jail. Eventually, this habitual sin cost him his wife, his baby and his ministry.

Involvement in the Occult

Occult involvement is another root of generational patterns. Seeking direction from sources other than God is an egregious affront to His sovereignty and holiness. The Bible is very clear as to God's position on occult involvement: "I will set my face against the person who turns to mediums and spiritists to prostitute himself by following them, and I will cut him off from his people" (Leviticus 20:6). Deuteronomy 18:10–13 puts it this way:

> Let no one be found among you who sacrifices his son or daughter in the fire, who practices divination or sorcery, interprets omens, engages in witchcraft, or casts spells, or who is a medium or spiritist or who consults the dead. Anyone who does these things is detestable to the LORD, and because of these detestable practices the LORD your God will drive out those nations before you. You must be blameless before the LORD your God.

All occult involvement brings spiritual confusion. This confusion prevents us from being able to pray, understand Scripture or hear God clearly. If our ancestors engaged in occult involvement, we need to be cut free from the influences that may affect us or our children.

The Rev. Patricia Smith, an authority on generational healing, explains that occult involvement often comes from a spiritual hunger to find God. Yet sometimes in the midst of trials and tribulations, instead of turning *to* God for help, individuals turn *away* from God and become involved in occult practices.

These practices include satanism, fortune-telling, seances, mind control, channeling and astrological charts. We will discuss these and others in chapter 9, "Healing of Occult Experiences." These things are an abomination to God and need to be renounced.

The concept of breaking our ties and bondage to Satan and the way he has infected the world is not new in our Christian tradition. In some sacramental denominations (Catholic, Episcopal, Lutheran), the language in the baptismal rite includes statements that "renounce Satan and all his works." For adult baptisms, the adult himself renounces these effects of Satan in the world. In infant baptisms, parents and godparents do this on behalf of the child. These baptismal words are traced back to the earliest traditions of the Church. Sadly, very little is explained today about the meaning of these words. Perhaps if we better understood the commitments we make for ourselves and our children and godchildren, less would be needed in the way of generational healing.

Unhealthy Relationships

When we are raised in dysfunctional homes, this becomes our example of how families relate to one another. Destructive patterns are set in place. If, for instance, daughters see their fathers habitually abuse their mothers, they begin to think that this is appropriate behavior in a marriage and may marry men who are abusive. This takes a toll on self-esteem; those who are chronically abused begin to feel that they deserve it or that it is their fault. If sons see this same abuse, they may believe that it is permissible to abuse their wives.

When praying once for a young woman who was repeatedly abused by her grandfather, I learned that her mother was also abused throughout her childhood. Her mother apparently thought nothing of leaving her daughter with this same abuser.

Curses

There is one obvious cause for destructive patterns in families and that is curses. This is not something we talk much about in America, but when traveling to places like India and Africa you soon realize that curses are taken very seriously in much of the world. Even when my family lived in England, people had an understanding about witches and curses that our culture here in the United States largely ignores.

Many times, I have prayed for people and felt they were under some type of curse. Several years ago, Christian Healing Ministries was involved in a medical study of arthritis patients with Dr. Dale Matthews, a research physician with the National Institute of Health Research. The study was held in Clearwater, Florida, and I was praying with a former church organist named Nancy.

Nancy's arthritis affected her the most in her legs and hips, and she walked with a cane. While praying for her, I kept hearing the Lord say she was under some sort of curse against her physical health. After a while, I asked her if anyone had ever wished her ill or had cursed her in any way.

She immediately said, "Yes, my sister-in-law!" and told me how she and her sister-in-law had gotten into a huge argument over Nancy's teenage daughter two years before. She said her sister-in-law screamed at her for two hours with vile and evil comments against both Nancy and her daughter. She was diagnosed with arthritis within six months of this incident.

Before praying, I asked Nancy where her pain level was on a scale of one to ten, with ten being the worst. She answered that it was a seven. She was having difficulty walking this particular day, having to rely heavily on her cane.

Laying my hand gently on Nancy's shoulder, I prayed a very simple prayer: "In the name of Jesus Christ, with the authority given to me as a Christian, I break Nancy free from any curse, hex or spell spoken against her by her sister-in-law. I render all words spoken against Nancy or her daughter null and void. I break Nancy and her daughter free from her sister-in-law physically, spiritually and emotionally. I place the cross and blood of Jesus between them. I pray for health and wholeness for Nancy's body, mind and spirit. Amen."

81

Immediately after praying, Nancy wanted to get up and walk to see if she could notice any difference. She was able to stand taller and walk without pain for the first time in weeks. In her excitement, Nancy did not want to use her cane, so I encouraged her to hold my arm as we walked. After walking back and forth, I asked her where the pain was on the pain scale. She answered, "A one!"

A year later at a reunion for the arthritis study, Nancy was still walking without her cane. She also had experienced a wonderful vacation that summer that required a lot of walking and climbing stairs. She looked terrific and truly felt that breaking the curse was an important part of her healing.

Curses can continue for generations. When we look at family lines, we often can see repeated patterns that could be the result of curses. For example, Father Marshall Lowell, an Episcopal priest who conducts generational healing Eucharists, is a huge advocate of generational healing. In his family, there was a repeated pattern of one male per generation dying at age 42, then 65, then 42 again. His father having died at 65, Marshall was delighted to discover generational healing when he was 41. He is now 55 and pleased to share this story with others.

Steps to Take

Praying for generational healing is like standing in the gap for our families and repenting of anything we know of that was not pleasing to God. It is also an opportunity to pray for cleansing from the destructive patterns that have affected us or our children and grandchildren.

Generational healing starts with identifying those patterns in our families that are outside the perfect will of God. These may be patterns of sickness (including mental, physical, emotional and spiritual disease), habitual patterns of sin (many of which are listed later in this chapter) and destructive or unhealthy relationships.

Then, once we have identified the patterns, we write them down on paper and present them to God. This can be accomplished in several ways. Some people offer them to God in prayer. Some people bring their lists to the altar when receiving Holy Communion. Many people burn the lists after they have been presented to God as a symbol of the release.

Dealing with these patterns is particularly meaningful at a service of Holy Communion. During the service the minister can include prayers specifically renouncing occult involvement, breaking of sins and patterns of sickness for those taking part. There is so much power in the Lord's Supper; when an emphasis is made during this special rite to include generational healing, much cleansing can occur.

It is particularly beneficial before taking Holy Communion to complete the occult sheet (see chapter 9) and to develop a family tree (discussed at the end of this chapter). This will target past occult involvement and emotional illnesses, sins and influences that may be passed down through family lines. In this way, you have a thorough understanding of the purpose of the Eucharist and its relation to generational healing as you participate in it.

As an Episcopalian, I highly recommend the beautiful liturgies found in *The Book of Common Prayer*. A minister can supplement the Eucharistic services found in that source, or the Communion wordings of any Christian tradition, with prayers such as the following.[1]

Prayer for the Renunciation of Occult Involvement

This prayer may be used in place of a sermon or at another appropriate place during the service:

1. These prayers are taken from the Rev. Patricia A. Smith's *From Generation to Generation: A Manual for Healing* (P.O. Box 14780, Jacksonville, Fla.: Jehovah Rapha Press, 1996), 200–201.

In the name of Jesus Christ, I repent of and renounce any and all satanic, occult, pagan or New Age practices in which I or any other member of my family line, past or present, may have been engaged.

I renounce, on behalf of myself and my family, direct satanic involvement, seeking knowledge or power from sources other than the Holy Spirit, seeking contact with the dead, playing games connected with the occult, occult organizations and religions, and any other practices that may involve spirits of the occult. In the mighty name of Jesus. Amen.

Prayer for the Affirmation of One's Faith

The following is from the *Book of Common Prayer.* I suggest it as a prayer of renunciation and affirmation of one's faith.

I renounce Satan and all the spiritual forces of wickedness that rebel against God. I renounce the evil powers of this world that corrupt and destroy the creatures of God. I renounce all sinful desires that draw me from the love of God. I turn to Jesus Christ and accept Him as my Savior. I put my whole trust in His grace and love. I promise to follow and obey Him as my Lord. Amen.

Prayer for Generational Healing

In the place of "The Prayers of the People" or any general service of prayer, the following litany, written specifically for the healing of generations, may be inserted:[2]

Celebrant: Almighty and everlasting God, please heal all hurts and free from all bondage all generations of our family lines, past, present and future.

2. This generational healing litany and the two prayers following it are taken from the Rev. Patricia A. Smith's book *From Generation to Generation: A Manual for Healing* (P.O. Box 14780, Jacksonville, Fla.: Jehovah Rapha Press, 1996), 148–50.

People: Lord, in Your mercy, hear our prayer.

Celebrant: We thank You for all those in our family lines who through their love and care passed down to us peace, love and an ability to know You and Your Son, Jesus Christ.

People: Lord, in Your mercy, hear our prayer.

Celebrant: We ask Your forgiveness of those in past generations who may have sinned against You and hurt others by engaging in occult practices, pagan and satanic worship, and all the abominations associated with these practices. Please break the hold these sinful practices have on our family lines.

People: Lord, in Your mercy, hear our prayer.

Celebrant: We ask Your forgiveness for those in past generations who may have sinned against You and hurt others by holding onto anger, unforgiveness and unrepentant bitterness. Please break the hold these sins have on our family lines.

People: Lord, in Your mercy, hear our prayer.

Celebrant: We ask Your forgiveness for those in past generations who may have sinned against You and hurt others by committing suicide, murder or abortion. Please break the hold these sins have on our family lines.

People: Lord, in Your mercy, hear our prayer.

Celebrant: We now commend into Your hands anyone in our family lines who committed suicide, was stillborn, was aborted, or died an untimely death, especially [insert names here]. Receive them into the arms of Your mercy, into the blessed rest of everlasting peace, and into the glorious company of the saints in light.

People: Lord, in Your mercy, hear our prayer.

Celebrant: We now offer our love and forgiveness to those who hurt members of our family lines. We also offer our love and forgiveness to those members of our family lines who sinned against others. We ask You to bring all these people into wholeness.

People: Lord, in Your mercy, hear our prayer.

Celebrant: We ask You to forgive those of us in this present generation and our descendants for any way in which we may have given in to the tendency to sin in the same way as our forebears did. Forgive us and restore us to life and health.

People: Lord, in Your mercy, hear our prayer.

Celebrant: We offer prayers for those family members who are in special need of Your healing touch. [Additional specific prayers can be inserted here.]

All: In the name of Jesus Christ and by the power of His cross and blood, we now break and make null and void any curses, contracts, covenants, hexes, spells or pacts made against our family lines, or made by any member of our family lines against another person. We break and make null and void any inner vows, bitter root judgments or expectations made against our family lines or by any member of our family lines against another person. We place the cross and blood of Jesus, the symbols of His power and authority, between the past generations of our families and the present generations, cutting off any evil that could be passed down. In the powerful name of Jesus. Amen.

Celebrant: Almighty Father, we ask that You reveal to us any places in our family lines that need further prayers. Break the bondage of sin and ignorance. Look upon all of the people in our generational lines with compassion. Free them all, that they might come before You in a sure knowledge of Your love and forgiveness. Send into every dark and hurting place the love of Your Son Jesus Christ, that all generations may learn to live in wholeness of mind, body and spirit, to the eternal glory of Your name, in and through Your Son, our Lord Jesus Christ. Amen.

In addition, the following practical steps may help you or those for whom you are praying:

1. Renounce anything contrary to the Lord.
2. Renew baptismal vows.
3. Ask Jesus to forgive your family for occult activity, habitual patterns of sin or destructive or unhealthy patterns of relationships.
4. Pray for healing of sins and weaknesses, and in place of them pray for the Holy Spirit to directly counteract the sin.
5. Personally forgive your ancestors for any of these activities or sins.
6. Ask forgiveness of yourself for any way you have judged your family or followed some of these patterns in your own life, perhaps influencing others.
7. Ask Jesus to come into the situations, showing Himself as Savior and Lord.
8. Realize that if some of the areas discussed above are severe or have existed for years, there may be a need to participate in more than one generational healing experience.

The two prayers below are helpful when praying for generational healing, particularly in areas of common family predispositions, such as alcoholism and common family sin patterns. I also have included a prayer of thanksgiving for blessings that have been passed down through the generations.

Prayer for the Healing of Generational Predispositions

Dear Lord, for the predisposition or sin to [name every predisposition or sin you know of] that has come down to me through my

87

mother, my father, my grandparents or any other family member, I ask You through Your power to set me free. Send Your Holy Spirit, and by the power of Your Holy Spirit and by the Sword of the Spirit cut me free from any predisposition or sin to [name them].

Lord Jesus, in place of this weakness, fill me with the power of Your Holy Spirit, and fill me with Your spirit of [name whatever fruit of the Spirit counteracts this weakness that you have, such as self-control, confidence, courage, fortitude]. Thank You, Lord, for healing me and my descendants. In Your precious name I pray. Amen.

Prayer for Healing of Generational Bondage

Heavenly Father, I come before You in the blessed name of Jesus and in the power of the Holy Spirit. I thank You for sending Jesus by whose holy blood and precious sacrifice I and my loved ones can be set free from the brokenness, woundedness, sinful attitudes and negative patterns of my ancestry. I thank You, Father, that You have called me to be free from all bondage in the name of Jesus, and I praise You that, in Christ, I shall be set free.

And now, Lord Jesus, gently reveal to me in the power of the Holy Spirit those ways in which I may be living out inherited sin patterns. All of these sin patterns, known and unknown to me, in my life and in the lives of my ancestors, in my spouse's life, in his/her ancestors and in our offspring, I acknowledge before You, Father. I confess to You the evil inclinations, compulsions and bad habits that have influenced us. I ask You to forgive me and all my ancestors, my spouse and his/her ancestors and our offspring for all these sins. In the name of Jesus and by His holy blood, set us free in You forever, Holy Father. Empty our souls of sin, and fill them with the holiness of Jesus.

I claim the Lord Jesus Christ as my true inheritance, and I thank You, Father, for the most wonderful gift of Your holy Son. I bless You, Jesus, that You have come to show me my true roots, *which are within the very heart of God the Father. I praise You, Holy Trinity. According to Your Word (John 8:36), those whom the Son sets free are free indeed. Alleluia! Amen.*

Prayer of Thanks for Generational Blessings

Dear Father, I thank You and praise Your holy name for the blessings of [list them all] that have been passed down to me through my family. I thank You for the faithfulness of those in my ancestry who were godly. I thank You that in any family, we find not only inherited sins for which we should seek forgiveness but also inherited blessings for which we can praise You. Thank You, Lord. Amen.

Preparation of Your Family Tree

A family tree can be very helpful in identifying common illnesses and sin patterns in a family and targeting those areas that may need concentrated prayer. A family tree is used to diagram family history so that you can see at a glance where problems are in each generation.[3]

Pray before filling out the family tree. Ask the Holy Spirit for guidance and direction in remembering family relationships and stories that have passed down through the generations.

Begin at the bottom of the tree; fill in your name and your spouse's name, and any problems you have (if divorced, insert your previous spouse's name, too). Do the same with your children, your parents and your brothers and sisters. Continue in this way up the family tree, as far as you can remember, indicating any patterns or problem areas in your family line. Some problems come down vertically, as from grandfa-

---

3. The list of generational problems and the family tree on p. 96 are adapted from the Rev. Patricia A. Smith's *From Generation to Generation: A Manual for Healing* (Jacksonville, Fla.: Jehovah Rapha Press, 1996), 141–142, 199.

ther to father, some horizontally, from aunt to aunt or cousin to cousin.

Some problems will be obvious; others are known only to God. Do not worry about what you do not know. Jesus will reveal what you need to know, and what He reveals He will bring into healing. Great traumas may be healed through generational healing prayer without your knowing their exact cause. However, if you find that your family's problems are not completely resolved after a healing prayer session or Holy Communion, continue to intercede about them. In some cases, it may be necessary for generational healing prayer to be repeated several times for one family line.

Go back at least four generations—even if you do not know all the names. If possible, check with parents, grandparents and other relatives to get more details or clearer information.

Depict the family tree graphically. A sample is included here for your reference.

Once you have finished constructing the family tree, look at possible patterns or problem areas within the family bloodlines. Below are some of the common areas of generational bondage or sin that may help jog your memory and make a more complete picture of your family line.

Remember to ask the Holy Spirit to reveal His truth. He may name something that is not listed below. It is essential to put down all areas revealed to you in order to break the patterns of generational sin.

Unusual or Violent Deaths

Identify, by name, the people in your family who:

- committed or attempted suicide
- were murdered or died in tragic ways such as accidents, wars (including POWs and MIAs) or violence
- had an abortion or participated in/sponsored an abortion

- had repeated miscarriages
- died in a mental institution, nursing home or prison, especially those who felt lonely, unloved and/or abandoned
- were not given a Christian burial, including committal services or prayer, or who were unmourned
- were unnaturally grieved
- experienced untimely deaths (for example, a pattern of males dying at an early age)

Evidence of Occult Activity, Demonic or Oppressive Spirits

Here is a partial listing. For a more complete list, see "The Occult Sheet" in chapter 9. Identify evidence of:

- superstitions
- involvement in the occult (for example, witchcraft, astrology, spiritualism or divination)
- opening one's self to powers of the spiritual realm, such as precognition or other psychic abilities
- severe trauma, with evidence of effects passed on through the family (for example, a drowning resulting in fear of water in other members, especially descendants)
- a blood covenant with Satan or involvement in satanic worship
- involvement with a witch or other persons involved in the occult

Habitual Patterns of Sin

These are numerous. Begin with sexual sins:

- adultery/fornication
- prostitution
- homosexuality, lesbianism

- incest
- pornography (homosexual, heterosexual or child)
- sexual perversions such as bestiality
- sexual promiscuity
- lust
- sexual addictions

Be sure to list all sexual partners as well as any soul-ties you have with another. A soul-tie is an unhealthy connection with another person. You allow the person to control you in certain areas. You begin to lose your individuality and self-confidence. You let the person make decisions for you, or you base your decisions on what you think the person wants you to do. If the person is really good at manipulation, you will think that he or she is spiritually superlative and will let him or her tell you what God is saying to you. The longer the unhealthy relationship, the stronger the soul-tie.

This is extremely important. Even if a long-term relationship was not sexual, you may be tied spiritually, emotionally or mentally. If you are enjoined to another, you must be cut free from this relationship. Remember that Jesus does not separate us from a person if we are tied to him or her in ways that are holy and within God's plan and will. He only cuts us free from the unholy or destructive part of the relationship. This is an especially important step when you are married or planning to marry. Your marriage bed should only include you, your spouse and God.

Other habitual sins include:

- violence
- abuse (physical, mental or emotional)
- incest
- racial prejudice
- anger
- religious prejudice

- murder
- pride
- greed
- materialism
- arrogance
- hatred
- unforgiveness or holding grudges

Destructive or Unhealthy Patterns of Relationships

Look for these traits in your family members:

- addictions (alcoholism, nicotine, drugs, food, etc.)
- divorce
- abuse (emotional, mental or physical)
- hostility
- control
- manipulation
- bondage (domination)
- revenge-seeking
- unforgiveness
- bitterness
- anger
- depression
- any person considered an outcast, reject or black sheep

Diseases and Predisposition to Illness

Again, here is a partial list of physical maladies. You may be aware of others.

- arthritis
- forgetfulness

- manic depressive disorders
- respiratory trouble
- cancer
- headaches
- mental retardation
- skin problems
- diabetes
- heart trouble
- mental disturbances
- ulcers
- depression
- high blood pressure
- nervous breakdowns

Historical Family Connections

This is broad-scale involvement in sin in which your family may have taken part.

- involvement with events of great sin, evil or trauma (for example, massacres, plagues, slavery, conquests)
- ethnic origin issues—negative traits, cultural evils, oppression, curses

Religious History

List all non-Judeo/Christian religions in the family or ancestral history.

In Utero Wounding

This is discussed at length in chapter 8. For now note the following:

- a child conceived through lust or rape
- illegitimacy
- parent considering adoption or abandonment
- ambivalence or rejection from either parent
- fears/anxiety (for example, mother had difficulty carrying child to term)
- attempted/failed abortion
- loss of father
- life-threatening illness of the mother
- life-threatening illness of the baby
- mother had miscarriage(s) or abortion before you were conceived

And Finally

As you meditate on all of these areas, ask the Lord where the problems that surface had their beginning. Offer them *all* to God for healing.

In conclusion, remember to:

Commit your family to the Lord.
Pray for protection.
Seek ministry for personal issues.

Family Tree

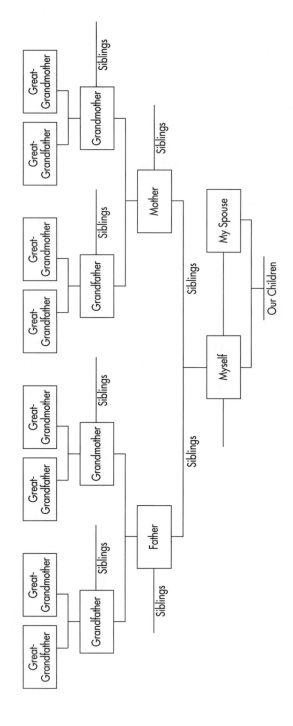

SIX

PHYSICAL HEALING

God created Adam and Eve in perfect health; sickness and disease did not exist in the Garden of Eden. Man was not created to die. Thus, we know that God's perfect will is for us to be healthy.

However, because Adam and Eve allowed sin to enter God's beautiful world, we all inherited the effects of sin—including sickness and death. And we are sinful creatures ourselves, as God's Word teaches us. Because of this, we are open to illnesses in our bodies, our minds and our spirits.

So what is the hope for us? As Christians, we recognize God's sovereign power. We know that He has power over sin, sickness and death. We know that if He chooses, He can and will heal. Thus, we pray for His merciful healing. We do not deserve it—none of us. But we know that He is a God of mercy and love.

Physical Healing Is a Mystery

Prayer for physical healing is prayer for a sickness caused by disease or accident. This type of prayer is probably the most common, as most people ask for prayer for physical problems before anything else.

The first thing I would like to share about physical healing is that it is a *mystery*. We never really know *whom* God is going to heal, or *when* He is going to heal, or even *how* He is going to heal. This may seem a little strange coming from someone who has been involved in the healing ministry for sixteen years, but it is truth.

It is actually because of my experience in the healing ministry that I do understand this as truth. My job is to pray for people for healing, and probably most often for physical healing. God's job is to heal. When or whom He chooses to heal, or the particular method by which He does the healing, is always a surprise to me. People involved in the healing ministry for many years also have grasped this valuable insight.

On some special occasions, God might tell someone that He is about to perform healing. In this situation an individual hears "a word of knowledge" from the Lord saying that a particular person is being healed or will be healed. It is exciting when this happens, as my friend Bob in Dublin, California, would agree.

While attending a prayer group of approximately 35 people at a Catholic church, Bob heard the Lord say that He wanted to heal a woman's eyes. He shared this out loud, and a woman with cataracts in both eyes stood and made her way forward. The leader asked Bob to pray for her since he was the one with the word of knowledge.

Bob looked into her face. Both eyes were thickly covered with a white film. As he placed his hands over her eyes, both he and she felt tremendous heat, and a chalky, milky liquid began running over Bob's hands and down her cheeks. When Bob removed his hands, he looked into beautiful blue eyes. Her vision was totally restored! Needless to say, the entire prayer group went crazy, laughing and praising God in delightful jubilation.

It is wonderful to be able to anticipate the work of the Lord and then see Him perform such a miracle. These are thrilling experiences and very encouraging when they happen, although most of the time we are not given any idea of God's plans.

And most healings I have seen have not been so dramatic. God heals different people differently. Some experience immediate healing, like this woman. Some experience partial healing, as when a tumor diminishes in size. Some receive no healing at all at the time of the prayer but wake up one morning a week later totally healed. And some are not healed at all.

Only God in His great wisdom knows what is going to happen to whom, when; and only He knows why He will or will not allow it to happen. As a prayer minister, I never have assurance that a person will be healed. My assurance is only in the goodness and wisdom of God my Father. I find that the only thing I am called to do is pray, allowing the healing power of God to move through me. The more a person tries to figure out the healing ministry, the more she realizes she does not understand. It is sort of like herding cats: It cannot be done.

When my father-in-law retired from a parochial ministry, he was eager to get involved in the healing ministry. He prayed and communicated this to the Lord and heard the Lord respond in this way: *Frank, I can really use you in the healing ministry if you can remember two important things. First, you don't have any answers. Second, you can't heal anyone. If you can remember these two things, we'll get along fine.*

This important message was passed along to me as I sat beside Father Frank and began praying for the physically ill. Little did I know that this same message would bring me to a deep and personal time of soul searching about my own future in the healing ministry. I thought I fully understood that healing was up to God. Then we were called to pray for two precious children.

It was in 1986. Christian Healing Ministries received a call asking if we could send a prayer team to a small town about an hour away. Two children from separate families were terminally ill and in need of prayer for physical healing. Don and Anne Bloch, two mighty prayer warriors on staff at this time, asked if I would like to travel down and pray with them.

The little boy, Adam, was five and suffering from cancer. The little girl, Vanessa, was seven and had lymphoma, another form of cancer. Anne, Don and I spent several hours praying for each of these children. We prayed out loud, we prayed silently and we used our prayer languages, meaning we prayed in tongues. We prayed by the "laying on of hands" and by "soaking prayer," both of which I will discuss later in this chapter.

We prayed absolutely every possible way that we knew. We used everything we had learned about physical healing prayer, and we tried praying with as much faith as possible. The families of these children were Christians, and they also were praying, along with their extended and church families. A tremendous amount of prayer was being directed toward the healing of these two beautiful children.

Six months later, we received a call that Adam had died and Vanessa was healed. How do we explain this? We really cannot explain it, even though many people try. Some may think, *Those people just didn't have enough faith,* or *God wanted Adam to experience the ultimate healing: going to heaven to live with Him.* If the latter is the answer, then why are we so uncomfortable saying the words *I don't know* when it comes to understanding what happened?

The truth is that we do not know or understand why God healed Vanessa and did not heal Adam. It is a mystery! This really upset me when it happened. I kept trying to figure it out and I could not! Over and over I thought, *I wonder what I did wrong?* Finally, I prayed and asked the Lord why He healed Vanessa and did not heal Adam, and I received an answer.

The Lord said, *Norma, you're going to last a lot longer in the healing ministry if you don't ask the* why *questions. You don't have to know the* why. *You don't have to know the* what. *You don't have to know the* when, *and you don't have to know the* where. *All you have to know is the* who, *and I am the great* Who!

He continued, *Sometimes I am going to give you one piece of a puzzle. Your job is to take that one piece and place it in the puzzle at the right time. It may be a beginning piece or an ending piece or it may be a piece in the middle. You are not to be concerned with the size of the piece or whether I give someone else two pieces or not. Your job is to take your piece and put it in at the right time.*

This is a lesson that I have continued to remember and share with others about this often misunderstood ministry. In fact, if we believe a person's physical healing is up to us, we will probably refuse to pray with them for fear that nothing will happen. It helps us to move forward when we accept the fact that we are not responsible for a person's healing. *However, we are responsible if we fail to pray.*

Overcoming Hesitancy about Praying for Healing

Through the years many people have asked me how I got started in the healing ministry. This question has several answers. I observed prayer teams at my church from a distance, read books by my father-in-law and read and believed the Scriptures about healing. But truthfully, the way I became involved in the healing ministry was by praying for my little dog, Butterscotch, who had arthritis.

For fourteen years, we had a precious little Peek-a-Poo (a Pekinese and poodle mix) that was greatly loved by our family, especially our five children. When he was about ten years old, I noticed he was beginning to walk more slowly and deliberately. He also on occasion had difficulty getting up. A trip to the vet confirmed arthritis and the sad news of a progressive disease. Like many people, I accepted the news with the idea that there was nothing I could do. As time progressed, Butterscotch walked more slowly, dragging his little legs.

101

One morning, as he dragged his left leg behind him, Butterscotch seemed to be in intense pain. I was overwhelmed with compassion. I thought about the healing Scriptures, and especially the one saying we "shall lay hands on the sick, and they shall recover" (Mark 16:18, KJV). I looked all around, thinking, *Well, Peter has gone to work and the kids are all at school. There isn't anybody else here, just me and the dog, so I can't look too foolish.*

I got down on the floor with Butterscotch and, placing my hands on his hips and back legs, I prayed, "Lord Jesus, Your Word says we are to lay hands on the sick and they will get better. I'm asking You to please pour Your healing power into Butterscotch and help him to walk better. You know, Lord, how much we love this dog and how much he means to our family. Thank You, Lord. Amen."

I noticed in the afternoon that Butterscotch was walking better and had more energy. I continued praying for my little dog, seeing improvement each time.

Many times what a person lacks is courage to begin. My experience with Butterscotch gave me the courage and encouragement to pray for myself when I had a headache or backache. I would place my hands on the affected area and ask for God's healing power to flow into and around the pain and discomfort.

The more I did this, the more relaxed I was with the process, eventually becoming comfortable praying with the children for their many injuries, pains and discomforts. After a while they would actually come to me saying, "Mommy, I have a headache. Please pray for my head." They learned that the first response for an illness or injury was healing prayer. I still remember Jason and Danny, my two younger sons, running in one day from elementary school with concern for their friend, saying, "Quick, Mommy, we have to pray! John fell off the monkey bars and broke both his arms!"

We need to remember that praying for healing is really very simple. It is holding a person up to the Lord and saying, "Lord

Jesus, please heal my friend, Jane. Please take her pain away and help her to feel better. Thank You, Lord. Amen."

We need not be worried about how much faith we have. Our faith needs to be in God and His goodness and faithfulness, not in our own faith. Our job is to pray; God's job is to heal. Remember, the Word says that "these signs shall follow them that believe" (Mark 16:17, KJV), and as "believers" we are to pray.

Every person feels a little shy and uncomfortable in the beginning. We feel this way whenever attempting something new and different. Think about the first time you hit a golf or tennis ball, danced the Electric Slide or drove a new and different car. The more we participate in a new activity, the more comfortable we become. The more we venture out into the unknown territory of physical healing prayer, the more we see God's extraordinary power working through His most ordinary creatures.

Jesus came to teach others and to heal, and He chose some ordinary characters as His companions. It was this motley crew that He chose to teach and instruct for a period of three years. These were the ones who carried on His ministry after He was gone. How interesting that He selected the people He did! They were not the highly respected religious people of the time, but common people like you and me.

Intercessory Prayer in Action

Thus, we see that the most important thing Christians can do in the area of physical healing is to pray, remembering that healing is up to God. Intercessory prayer, or praying *for* someone, is extremely beneficial.

We have many examples of intercession in the Bible, beginning in the Old Testament. For example:

"For the sake of his great name the LORD will not reject his people, because the LORD was pleased to make you his own.

103

As for me, far be it from me that I should sin against the LORD by failing to pray for you."

1 SAMUEL 12:22–23

Jesus, of course, is our perfect example of intercession. He intercedes for us constantly. If our desire is to become more like Him, let us recognize His model of prayer:

Because Jesus lives forever, he has a permanent priesthood. Therefore he is able to save completely those who come to God through him, because he always lives to intercede for them.

HEBREWS 7:24–25

Our commitment as Christians to this task of intercession is vital to healing. Intercessory prayer is the tool that we, as Christians in God's army, are given and can use to fight the spiritual battles to which He calls us.

When JoAnn Buttner found a lump in her breast, her daughter, Ann, and I were very concerned. Ann, my prayer partner for many years, had prayed with me when my mother went through breast cancer. (She has been a breast cancer survivor since 1994.) We knew the importance of spending time together, interceding for JoAnn about her upcoming appointment with a surgeon.

A week after that appointment, JoAnn wrote this about her experience:

For over two years I have had pain in my upper back along and above the bra line, radiating through the back part of my arm. The doctors kept saying it was arthritis. I had been given different anti-inflammatory medicine and pain medication with no positive results for relief of pain. I must have tried 25–30 bras, thinking the bras were causing the pain. Before receiving prayer, I was in severe pain, especially at night interfering with sleep.

I was scheduled to see an orthopedic doctor for a bone scan, as bone cancer had become a concern. Then, I found a lump in my breast and made an appointment with a surgeon to discuss the next step. My daughter, Ann, and Norma prayed together for me while I was with the doctor.

A few days later, I realized all the pain in my back was gone. When I called Ann and told her about it, she told me that she and Norma had prayed not only for the lump in my breast, which turned out to be benign, but for any other physical problems that may trouble me. I was thankful to God. I was thankful that Ann and Norma prayed for me. I feel so much better.

The literal meaning of intercession is "the lightning of God reaching the mark." The Hebrew root of our word *intercession* is *pagah,* which means "to strike the mark." It is a warfare term. So when we use the word *intercession,* we are literally talking about warfare.

God desires to strike the mark through His believers, who are the light of the world. Jesus said:

> "You are the light of the world. A city on a hill cannot be hidden. Neither do people light a lamp and put it under a bowl. Instead they put it on its stand, and it gives light to everyone in the house. In the same way, let your light shine before men."
>
> MATTHEW 5:14–16

We need to hear the heart of our Father and release His light into our world through prayer.

Praying by Word and Touch

The New Testament teaches two main methods of prayer for physical healing. The first is praying by using the spoken *word* and the second is by praying with physical *touch.* Many times, people use a combination of these.

105

Word Prayers

The first type of word prayer is one we are most comfortable praying. It is the prayer of entreaty. This is an asking prayer, a humble prayer. We pray: "Lord Jesus, please heal my friend Mary."

With this type of prayer, we come to the Lord with our concern for this particular person and we ask that He heal him or her. We remember Jesus' words:

> "So I say to you: Ask and it will be given to you; seek and you will find; knock and the door will be opened to you. For everyone who asks receives; he who seeks finds; and to him who knocks, the door will be opened."
>
> LUKE 11:9–10

Along with our asking, we are taught to pray specifically. For instance, King David enjoins us to "pray for the peace of Jerusalem" (Psalm 122:6) and then suggests what specifically to pray for.

It helps to pray as specifically as possible with the prayer of entreaty. More healing seems to take place when we are specific. For instance, let's say Marty has a knee problem that affects his walking, and with it he experiences a great deal of pain and discomfort. When praying for Marty, you might pray something like: "Lord Jesus, we thank You for Marty's life. We hold Marty up to You now, Lord, and ask that You draw out this pain in his knee. We ask, Lord, that You alleviate the swelling, the pain and the discomfort, so he can walk more easily. Please improve his walking, Lord. We thank You and praise You. Amen."

One of the best prayers of entreaty I have heard is one spoken by Andrew, my little grandson, when expressing concern about his two-year-old sister, Avery. "Dear Jesus, Sissy threw up. Please heal her tummy. Thank You, Jesus. Amen."

Another type of word prayer is a prayer of authority or prayer of command. We see this in Luke's gospel when Jesus healed Simon's mother-in-law: "Now Simon's mother-in-law was suffering from a high fever, and they asked Jesus to help her. So he bent over her and rebuked the fever, and it left her" (Luke 4:38–39).

We also see this same prayer of authority or prayer of command in Mark's gospel with the man who was deaf and unable to speak:

> There some people brought to him a man who was deaf and could hardly talk, and they begged him to place his hand on the man. After he took him aside, away from the crowd, Jesus put his fingers into the man's ears. Then he spit and touched the man's tongue. He looked up to heaven and with a deep sigh said to him, "Ephphatha!" (which means, "Be opened!"). At this, the man's ears were opened, his tongue was loosened, and he began to speak plainly.
>
> MARK 7:32–35

When we first begin praying for others, the prayer of entreaty is the best place to start. After becoming more comfortable with praying and seeing results, we begin to sense when it might be more appropriate to "rebuke" the fever or "command" the sickness to leave, which is a more authoritative prayer. We see Jesus often praying with the prayer of authority, but remember that Jesus was in such close communion with His Father, He knew exactly how and when to pray.

We are probably most comfortable with the prayer of authority when we have been given a word of knowledge by God about the situation. For example, my husband, Peter, was traveling by plane and heard a baby crying. The Lord spoke to him, saying, *Go back and stand near the baby and pray for his ears.* Peter is a shy person and not one to draw attention to himself, but because he knew God was speaking to him, he obeyed immediately. Walking back to where the baby

107

was seated, he prayed a quiet prayer of authority for the pain to leave the baby's ears. The crying ceased immediately. Peter had confidence that healing would occur because of God's specific direction.

The prayer of authority is particularly effective when praying for cancer. Pray: "In the name of Jesus, I command these cancer cells to wither up and die. I rebuke these cancer cells and speak health and wholeness to this body." This is a prayer I have been praying regularly with Dan, who has lymphoma. I lay hands on his lungs where the cancer nodules are located and pray this prayer. I also pray for his immune system to be strengthened and for the chemotherapy to attack only the unhealthy cancer cells.

Many people are not comfortable praying a prayer of authority or prayer of command for physical healing, especially not in the beginning. If this is how you feel, don't worry. It usually comes after years of praying with people for physical healing, or when God seems to impart a special confidence to a person in a particular situation.

Praying with Touching

The second method of prayer for physical healing is physical touch. Love and concern are often communicated through touching. We hold a person's hand or put a comforting arm around someone who is suffering emotionally as well as physically. When hurting, a child comes to the loving parent to have "boo boos" kissed away, seeking solace and comfort in the arms of love and security.

This is where the traditional Christian practice of "the laying on of hands" enters the picture. As Christians, we know that God lives within us; Jesus taught us this at the Last Supper. And when Jesus gave the Great Commission, He said that those who believe will lay their hands on the sick and they will get well (see Mark 16:18).

When we lay hands on someone with the love of God and the express intent of bringing the person before God, he or she experiences more than just our human love. It is God's healing love that is being communicated. Often we hear comments like: "I feel the love of God flowing through me when you lay hands on me and pray. It feels so wonderful. It's as though Jesus is touching me and filling me with love!" This is also why Christians should try to be as "sin free" as possible, so the love of God can flow through us into a hurting world, one person at a time.

A friend of mine, who is a neuro-muscular massage therapist, takes the laying on of hands very seriously. Each morning, she comes in early, checks her schedule and prays for each client by name. She especially asks that God will use her to heal His people. Praying quietly through the work day, she asks God to use her touch to transmit His love and minister to her clients.

We must be careful, though, to be considerate when using this method of prayer. It is an essential element of praying for physical healing that the recipient of prayer feel safe and comfortable. Some people, especially those with a history of abuse, may be nervous about any invasion of their personal space. It is very important to ask permission before touching someone who is receiving prayer.

If it meets with the person's approval, try to lay hands on or near the area needing prayer. If, for instance, you are praying for someone's back, ask him to place your hands on the affected area, right on the spot where he experiences pain or discomfort. If the affected area is a private part of a person's body, simply lay your hands as close to that area as is appropriate, without invading the person's privacy or giving any cause for discomfort or concern to either of you. In some instances you might prefer to ask the prayer recipient to place his or her hand on the area that needs prayer and then place your hand on his or hers.

Gaining permission before laying hands on a person is especially important if you are in a public place such as a hospital or if you are praying in small groups or prayer teams. Actually, I have found that a team of two to pray and lay hands on an individual, though they may be supported by many others who are also praying, is very beneficial, as we see demonstrated in Scripture. Jesus gave us this example by sending the disciples out in pairs. "Calling the Twelve to him, he sent them out two by two and gave them authority over evil spirits" (Mark 6:7).

There are two other points to remember. One, it is helpful to explain to the person why laying hands on the specific area is beneficial. And, two, consider that this may be a person's first healing prayer experience and he or she may be nervous, not knowing what to expect.

James, the brother of Christ and one of the leaders of the early Church in Jerusalem, wrote his letter to Christians everywhere to help teach them practical aspects of Christianity. In it, he gives us the model we seek to emulate:

> Is any one of you sick? He should call the elders of the church to pray over him and anoint him with oil in the name of the Lord. And the prayer offered in faith will make the sick person well; the Lord will raise him up. If he has sinned, he will be forgiven. Therefore confess your sins to each other and pray for each other so that you may be healed. The prayer of a righteous man is powerful and effective.
>
> JAMES 5:14–16

Look at this teaching at work in the experience of my friend Larry Flanagan who suffered a massive heart attack at work. With a blood clot broken loose and lodged in Larry's heart, he was rushed into emergency. His wife, Shloe, and a prayer team gathered quickly outside the emergency room, interceding and singing hymns.

As Larry went into cardiac arrest, the team kept praying— for Larry's life to be spared, for the doctors, the nurses, the equipment. As they prayed outside, Larry's heart stopped for two to three minutes. He was dead. The doctors zapped his chest with paddles, and the team kept praying, both in English and in their prayer languages. Larry came back. As the doctors worked to stabilize him, the prayer team praised God with hymns and spiritual songs. And then for a second time Larry's heart stopped. More prayer by his wife and prayer team. Again, he was resuscitated and stabilized. More praise and thanksgiving to God. They lost him a third time. Prayer, intercession for Larry's heart and the doctors' hands continued. Again, he was resuscitated. This time he was stabilized for three to four hours.

During this period of time, many more people were notified and enveloped Larry and Shloe in prayer. Intercessors were being called all over the country. Priests, friends and colleagues were coming to the hospital to join in prayer. Larry went into cardiac arrest for the fourth time. Again, more intercessory prayer, beseeching God to pour His healing power into Larry's heart and body. Again, Larry stabilized and finally was placed in intensive care.

Days turned into weeks as his devoted wife sat by his bed praying specifically for each physical abnormality resulting from the heart attack. Literally hundreds of people were praying for Larry, many interceding from miles away, as well as teams of rotating people in intensive care. As Larry lay in a coma, ministers and prayer teams joined Shloe in praying with the laying on of hands for the affected areas. For instance, since there had been a lack of oxygen to his brain, they prayed for the healing of any brain damage. When Larry was later diagnosed with edema, they prayed specifically for the fluid to be released and the swelling to go down. Both of Larry's doctors were Christians, and they also joined in the prayers.

After several weeks, things began to look very bad. Thirteen areas of Larry's body became compromised as he battled death. As he struggled to breathe on a ventilator, he experienced paralyzed lungs, kidney failure and a staph infection throughout his body, which caused a diabetic coma, high fever and pneumonia. Eventually, he was bleeding from every orifice of his body. The doctors told Shloe to call in the family. She did, as friends and colleagues again called in the intercessors and prayer teams.

As masses were offered and rosaries were prayed (the Flanagans are Lutheran), Larry was again encircled with prayer from literally hundreds of people from various denominations. As they infused Larry with five units of packed red blood cells and two units of whole blood, he continued to bleed from the pores of his body. An Episcopal priest came to administer Holy Communion, but Larry could not take the bread into his mouth. As Shloe pressed the host (bread) to Larry's lips, his blood covered it. At this point, his beloved wife took the bread, placed it into her own mouth and prayed, "Lord, I'm awfully tired. If you want him, go ahead and take him."

It was from this very time, this time of relinquishment, that Larry started to improve. He is alive and well today, years later, ministering healing prayer to others alongside his faithful wife. One doctor calls him "Miracle Man." Another says, "It was a miracle you survived at all." Larry says, "I'm alive today because of God's intervention. Prayer is a very powerful tool to be used when someone is ill or in a terminal condition."

Shloe says, "I believe totally in prayer, not just physically. No prayer goes unanswered. When you pray, there is always healing in some way. No prayer is ignored by God. When you lay hands upon a person, anoint him and lift him up in prayer—those prayers are answered. The Lord heals, whether you see it or not."

A little postscript to Larry's healing. He had been to the optometrist before the heart attack and had new glasses. After the heart attack, he could not see anything out of these glasses. He went back to his optometrist and was given another eye exam. The doctor said, "No wonder you can't see. Your glasses are too strong." Not only did God save his life, but He totally healed His vision! "Immediately he received his sight and followed Jesus, praising God. When all the people saw it, they also praised God" (Luke 18:43).

Prayer for Physical Healing Takes Time

The amount of time spent praying for an individual for physical healing is important. The longer we pray, the more we see happen. This is what the term *soaking prayer* means—praying often and for long periods of time for specific areas of the body that need healing.

Approximately ten years ago, I was praying at an evening healing prayer service for a woman with a neck tumor. The tumor was about the size of a golf ball and was on the right side of her neck. Her doctor, who was a Christian, had sent her to us for prayer before he operated later in the week. There was growing concern that this condition would affect her speech.

Laying my hands on her neck, I prayed for approximately five minutes. Nothing much seemed to happen. In other words, the tumor still felt hard and the size of a golf ball. I felt the Lord prodding me, *Keep praying. Don't stop.* After another ten minutes of prayer, I felt the tumor beginning to soften and shrink under my fingers.

We stopped for a moment and had her check it. Both she and the others on the prayer team felt that the tumor seemed smaller, as though it was softening and dissipating. We thanked the Lord and kept praying for another five to ten minutes. I kept feeling it getting smaller and smaller under my hand.

After about thirty minutes of continuous soaking prayer, the tumor was reduced to the size of a small marble. This was a dramatic change. In addition, she left feeling tremendously loved by God and peaceful about her upcoming surgery. Her doctor later told me the surgery had been a "chip shot" because the tumor was so reduced in size and no longer threatening her vocal cords. Both doctor and patient were overjoyed with the outcome.

Praying for long periods of time and praying often are most beneficial when praying for physical healing. The "name it and claim it" types of results to healing prayer, so publicized by the media, have not been my experience. With serious illnesses such as multiple sclerosis, cancer and arthritis, hours of prayer over an extended period of time may be necessary. Some find this to be boring or not very exciting, but I find it peaceful to enter with a team member into the healing presence of God.

When praying for physical healing, most of the time we see some degree of improvement. I would estimate that if we pray for one hundred people, we see approximately 10 percent totally healed, 80 percent with some improvement and another 10 percent with no change. These likely need another type of healing first, like inner healing, generational healing or renouncing the occult before the physical healing takes place. We will discuss this in a moment.

It helps to make a general assessment of the condition before beginning to pray for physical healing. By that I mean asking a few simple questions. I start with this: "On a scale of one to ten, with ten being excruciating pain, where is your pain level at this time?" After praying for about five minutes, I pause and ask the question: "Is it better, worse or the same?" If it is better, I ask: "How much better? Is it a little better or a lot better?"

This helps me to ascertain what is transpiring and the amount of healing taking place. It also informs me when I need to continue praying, using the soaking prayer method. Then after a few minutes I ask again: "Where is the pain on the scale of one to ten?" I continue praying until I see reasonable improvement or feel that another avenue should be explored.

The Need for Other Types of Healing

When after some time of prayer no physical healing seems to be taking place, or there is only marginal improvement, other possibilities should be considered. One of these is the need for emotional healing, a subject that we will discuss at length in the next chapter. There is often a connection between these two components. I have seen many people healed physically *after* they experienced emotional, or inner, healing. Barbara is a good example of this.

A friend of mine whom I affectionately refer to as "Saint Emma" brought Barbara to me about twelve years ago. Emma is one of those rare people who seek God every day with the express purpose of not only hearing Him clearly but being obedient to what she hears.

Barbara, having no car and no license, could not get to her appointments with us on her own. Emma picked her up and faithfully brought her to Christian Healing Ministries for her weekly appointments. This was not for one or two weeks but for a period of two years!

While Barbara and I had our prayer appointments, Emma took care of Barbara's two preschool daughters, reading and playing and taking them to the park. (See why I call her Saint Emma?)

When Barbara and I first began praying, the presenting problems were depression and chronic back pain due to scoliosis or curvature of her spine. Not only did Barbara suffer from physical depression that rendered her unable to care for herself, but a heaviness hung over her. She was extremely beaten down by life.

Barbara was sexually abused by her natural father and then again by her stepfather and stepbrothers. This went on throughout her childhood. She was never able to escape it, no matter where she lived. Her belief system was that women were subservient to men.

She remembers her stepfather coming home drunk at night with a gun and coming into the area where Barbara slept with her older sister. In a drunken rage, he would point the gun above the heads of the two girls and then fire off several rounds. She remembers the bullets flying over her head, boring into the headboard of her bed, as she shook and trembled

115

under the covers. She used to grab her sister and run out into the yard, hiding so they would be safe.

After a night like this one, she would try to rise in the morning, dress herself and her sister, and go to school. Is it any wonder she did not excel in school and never graduated from high school?

In our prayer sessions, Barbara spent an enormous amount of time forgiving her various family members. Along with this we spent many hours praying for emotional healing, allowing the Lord Jesus into the memories of abuse and trauma. We continued to pray for physical healing and began to see improvement in her back pain.

On the day Barbara dealt with the last person she needed to forgive and experienced Jesus' peace in those memories, we prayed again for her back. That day, as my hands were extended across her spine, I felt the vertebrae begin to move and line up. With the pain leaving and her spine moving into a straight position, Barbara began to cry tears of thankfulness and joy.

Emma, returning that day, was met with an exuberant Barbara. Opening the door, Barbara flung herself into Emma's arms exclaiming, "Emma, I'm healed! Emma, I'm healed!"

After Barbara's physical and emotional healing, she was able to achieve two of her lifelong dreams. First, she entered night school and received her Graduate Equivalency Degree. Second, Emma taught her to drive and took her for her driving test. On the day she passed her test, they came immediately to see me and proudly displayed her license.

Barbara became an active and concerned parent, participating in her children's school activities. She taught Sunday school in her church and spent Saturdays doing home evangelism visits. She loves sharing her testimony with others.

I later saw Barbara working at a sandwich shop, where she was laughing with her fellow employees. She was wearing a T-shirt that said "Jesus—the Way, the Truth and the Life."

Emotional healing was an important aspect in Barbara's overall healing. It seems that God will often delay physical healing so that a person can experience healing in other important areas first. God is on the side of life, and He is interested not just in our bodies but also in our minds and our spirits. He wants us to be well spiritually, emotionally, mentally and physically.

Generational healing is another contributing factor to physical healing. Some physical problems have a genetic predisposition that may need to be broken, especially in areas such as cancer, arthritis and heart disease. Many people experience physical healing after they have participated in prayer for the healing of their family's generations.

Doctors told Bessie, a prayer minister at Christian Healing Ministries, that she had a lump in her left breast and that surgery was recommended. Her mother had died of breast cancer. After we prayed for generational healing and breast cancer specifically, and Bessie received the laying on of hands, the lump disappeared and there was no need for surgery.

Occult involvement is also a major block to physical healing and must be renounced before much change takes place. This is true for both generational and individual involvement.

While playing on a bowling league, Nancy began to experience swelling and pain in her fingers. As an experienced pharmaceutical representative, Nancy knew she needed to have these symptoms checked out by a rheumatologist. After testing, she was diagnosed with rheumatoid arthritis, the same debilitating disease experienced by her aunt and great-grandmother.

Other symptoms Nancy experienced were inflammation, weakness, paralysis, extreme fatigue and depression. She found it difficult opening doors and asked Jesus every day to give her strength as she carried her heavy pharmaceutical bag from hospitals to doctors' offices.

While being treated by a rheumatologist, Nancy took anti-inflammatory drugs and started on methotrexate for prevention of bone destruction, which caused a number of side effects. These side effects of hair loss, skin problems and

117

extreme fatigue, coupled with the monthly blood tests, drastically modified her quality of life.

Nancy was reluctant to share with others about her arthritis because in her experience people were quick to judge: "If you have rheumatoid arthritis, you'll be on disability before too long." Attending an arthritis support group proved equally discouraging for her. She said, "As I walked into my one and only meeting, I found that the people were nice but in terrible shape. So many of them had severe deformities and most were on disability. I thought, *I don't want to come here. I don't want to give up.* I'm not taking away from the value of support groups, but I was in no way ready to receive the help they have to offer."

Her doctor reminded her that rheumatoid arthritis was an autoimmune disease that is both progressive and debilitating. After suggesting Nancy change her medical bag to one on wheels, he mentioned the fact that she was still wearing high heels. Before Nancy could answer, he handed her a prescription for orthopedic shoes. She accepted the prescription but thought with great indignation, *I'm not giving up my heels. I'm in my thirties and I am not wearing orthopedic shoes!*

Now before you judge Nancy for being in denial, you need to hear the rest of her story. By her own admission, Nancy did not see herself as an active Christian in her twenties and early thirties, even though she had received a personal call on her life. She had two dreams, one in which she saw Jesus on the cross, and a second in which Jesus spoke to her saying, *Proclaim My Word and serve Me.* Nancy attended mass each Sunday. However, she was obsessed about her future and constantly visited tarot card readers and delved into a variety of other occult activities.

After three years of living with the arthritis, Nancy went with her mother on vacation in Hawaii and attended a Catholic charismatic mass. Nancy said that while she was experiencing the prayer and praise, "I felt the presence of the Holy Spirit. There was such a heavy anointing at this church.

I turned to my mom and said, 'When I go home, I'm going to find a charismatic prayer group that will pray for healing.'"

After returning home, Nancy found that her church, St. Joseph's Catholic Church, actually had a charismatic prayer group that met for praise, worship and healing. She started going on a regular basis and asked for the laying on of hands for healing of her arthritis. During this time, the Lord spoke to her in her sleep. One night she heard Him clearly speak these words: *I am Jehovah—I AM, I AM. Look at Me. Look at Me!* Nancy says she knew immediately that the Lord was saying not to look at anything else about her future. She was to trust Him and Him alone.

After this experience, Nancy began cleaning her house of anything related to the occult. She destroyed all astrology charts, books and fortune-telling articles. She also prayed and asked the Lord to forgive her for looking to anything besides Him. After this, Nancy experienced yet another dream where choirs of angels were singing and celebrating. About this experience, Nancy said, "The Lord has been very good to me. He has been very faithful. He has given me dreams and visions. He confirmed to me that He was very happy that I saw the truth and acted on it right away. I didn't hesitate. I was convicted and said, 'Please forgive me.'"

From that day forward, Nancy began seeing tremendous improvement in her physical condition. She continued going to her charismatic prayer group, attended mass two or three times weekly and began coming to Christian Healing Ministries. The first time she came, a team prayed with her for back pain, and it was completely alleviated! This is where I met Nancy. After hearing about her occult history and generational predisposition to arthritis and praying with her about how to proceed in her healing, I felt sure that a generational healing Eucharist—service of Holy Communion—was in order.

This led to more physical improvement. She also was feeling better spiritually. She was able to hear the Lord more clearly and felt more connected to God the Father. As we con-

119

sidered these changes, we prayed continually for God to reveal anything else He wanted us to do. During this time, we felt that Nancy was to continue attending generational Eucharists monthly, come for individual appointments for emotional healing, attend sacramental services two to three times weekly and receive as much soaking prayer as possible. Remember that soaking prayer is continual prayer for long periods of time on specific joints or areas of the body.

During the emotional healing sessions, we asked the Lord to walk back through a number of memories where stressed-out Nancy made wrong choices in her life, and especially to cut her free from specific friends who were involved in the occult. Again, we saw considerable improvement in the joints, knees, ankles, fingers and wrists.

The Lord also revealed the stress and anger Nancy felt when her father died, and how compromised her immune system was in the loss of her beloved "Daddy." Nancy felt sure that the anger and the rheumatoid arthritis were connected. As we prayed through the memories of her father's illness and death, asking the Lord to lift the anger from her heart, mind and body, tremendous results again occurred in Nancy's physical and spiritual health.

As Nancy's arthritis became more improved, she heard God say during her prayer time as well as in another dream that He would heal her completely. In addition to hearing these words in her dream, she also saw herself laying hands on other people and praying for their healing.

Nancy says, "I knew God was going to heal me. I knew I was supposed to keep praying and waiting for it to happen." In April 1999, Nancy spent a day receiving soaking prayer from several prayer ministers. During this time, the Lord spoke these words: *Seek Me first in all things, and the rest shall follow. I lift all your cares and worries. I bless all My children abundantly. I make whole. I heal. I heal. My child, stay close to Me and listen. Be obedient always. Do not attach yourself to the things*

*of this world. Seek only Me, and the rewards that I have for you
in eternal life.*

Nancy says, "At that point I had a vision of Jesus and the
crown of thorns. I saw the blood flowing and Jesus said: *I gave
up My life to set captives free. Touch My hem. Touch My hem. I
come to heal. I am here with you, My child, always near, always
here. Stay close in My embrace.*"

Nancy's arthritis continued to improve until the symptoms
disappeared. No longer were her days racked with pain,
swelling, inflammation or fatigue. She has a closet full of high
heels and enjoys wearing them when calling on doctors and
medical clinics with her drug samples. By January 2001,
Nancy had been off all medication for a period of two years
and was totally pain free. During her last yearly checkup, the
tests for arthritis showed everything within normal range.
Today, Nancy is an active prayer minister and prays for others for healing.

While interviewing Nancy, I inquired if she had something
she wanted to share with the readers. She responded, "Jesus
loves you very much. Give Him all your cares and worries.
Open up your heart and let Him in, for He wants to bless you
abundantly."

Prejudices and Expectations about Physical Healing

As praying Christians, we must ask God to reveal any prejudices we might have about the healing ministry. Some of
these prejudices, for instance, might be a result of "faith heal-
ers" viewed on television and the style in which they operate.
We must seek God's forgiveness for judgments made against
these and any other individuals who seem to hamper our faithfulness to pray.

Some people believe that sickness is a cross sent from God
and that we should accept it as God's will and not pray for
healing. This thinking does not line up with Scripture, where

121

we see Jesus healing all who were brought to Him with sickness and diseases. "Jesus went through all the towns and villages, teaching in their synagogues, preaching the good news of the kingdom and healing every disease and sickness" (Matthew 9:35).

Others believe that it takes a saint to work a miracle. The Scriptures say nothing about being saintly or worthy. Mark's gospel says simply: "These signs will accompany those who believe" (Mark 16:17). The condition here is only that we believe.

We must make sure our faith is in God—not in our own faith. If you are struggling with the area of faith, you must do three things:

1. Confess your struggle to the Lord.
2. Pray for more faith and courage.
3. Pray for faith in God and His promises.

Many believe that healing comes as a result of the miraculous, and therefore physical healing is extraordinary, not a part of everyday living. Jesus never referred to healing as miracles. In fact, He referred to His healings as "works," making them quite ordinary occurrences.

Remember that whether or not a person receives healing and to what extent is not up to us. As Christians, our job is to lay hands on the sick and pray. God's job is to heal.

SEVEN

EMOTIONAL, OR INNER, HEALING

The Spirit of the Sovereign LORD is on me, because the LORD has anointed me to preach good news to the poor. He has sent me to bind up the brokenhearted, to proclaim freedom for the captives and release from darkness for the prisoners, to proclaim the year of the LORD's favor and the day of vengeance of our God, to comfort all who mourn, and provide for those who grieve in Zion.

ISAIAH 61:1–3

Memories can wound, cripple and bind people. They can keep us in bondage and prevent God's healing power from working in us. God's love, however, can transform our emotions and even our memories to set us free and allow us to live an abundant life through Christ.

Judith MacNutt tells a wonderful story about emotional, or inner, healing. I believe this story, which follows, explains the dynamics of how our memories can cripple and bind us.

An elephant trainer is giving a man a tour of the zoo. They come to the elephant house. Here the man notices that a large elephant has a chain around one ankle, which is staked in the ground at the other end. The chain is short and the links are thin. It is not a strong chain.

The man asks the trainer, "I've always been curious how such a small chain holds such a large animal."

The trainer replies, "Well, it doesn't. That chain is certainly not strong enough to bind him, but the elephant doesn't know that." And the man asks the trainer to explain.

The trainer continues, "When an elephant is first born, we take a chain and place it around his ankle and stake it in the ground. A newborn elephant weighs approximately two hundred pounds. He pulls and pulls, but he cannot break the chain or pull the stake out of the ground.

"As he grows, we keep using the same chain he had when he was first born. By the time he is full-grown, he is still being held by the same chain. But it is not the chain that is holding the elephant: *It's the memory of the chain.*"

This is a vivid illustration of inner woundedness. Hurtful memories are like the chain holding the elephant: They have the potential to keep us in bondage. These memories are not limited to events of childhood; they can reflect more recent events.

Let us begin our understanding of how the Lord brings emotional healing from these events with an example of a young woman and the memory that left her all but incapacitated.

A Case Study

My daughter-in-law, Vicki, came to hear me speak once on inner healing. After my talk, she described a young woman she was representing as a client. Vicki was the plaintiff's attorney in a case against an insurance company.

Vicki said that the young woman had been robbed and beaten while on duty managing an apartment complex and she

124

was experiencing tremendous fear and anxiety as a result. She said her client was a Christian and asked if I would consider seeing her and perhaps praying with her for inner healing.

Several weeks later, a young woman named Donna, a single mother of two, sat in my office and shared how an incident two years before had destroyed her life. Her hands shook as she spoke. I could see the pain, sorrow and fear etched on her face from the last two years.

I also sensed darkness over her, which I have learned to identify as spiritual oppression. This is a heaviness that seems to push people down, making them feel tired, discouraged, depressed and sometimes hopeless. This is the story that began to unfold.

Donna was in the office of the apartment complex when a man burst through the door with a gun. His behavior was hyper, possibly due to drugs, and he began screaming obscenities as he rushed at her. Donna had no doubt that he was going to kill her.

He grabbed her and clutched at her throat. Holding the loaded gun to her head, he hissed words into her ear: "I'm going to blow your [deleted] head off!" Donna was paralyzed with fear.

He proceeded to beat her on the head with the gun and then threw her across the desk, injuring her back. He kept saying he was going to kill her, but eventually he robbed her and left.

She was left in a crying heap, writhing in pain on the floor.

The police came and she was transported to the state hospital for treatment. A hospital psychiatrist was called in to question her about the emotional trauma. The manner in which Donna answered the questions led him to believe she might be a danger to herself or others.

In came two attendants in white coats who physically forced her into a straitjacket and transported her to the psychiatric unit for observation. This began two years of massive doses of antidepressant and anti-anxiety drugs to help Donna function.

She saw a psychiatrist three times a week in the beginning and was still seeing him once a week at the time she came to see me. I will never forget a comment Donna made about her many visits with her psychiatrist. She said that every time she tried to talk about her disappointment with God and where He was during all of this, the psychiatrist cut her off. He always said, "No, no. We don't talk about religion here."

Other than some help from a few Christian friends, this poor young woman had to work through all the tough spiritual issues on her own. Through prayer she had somehow reached the place of peace with God.

In addition, she prayed hard for God to help her forgive the man who had beaten and robbed her. She had actually been praying for him for the past six months! But even though she had come this far, she was still incapacitated by fear.

Donna stayed locked in her house with the blinds drawn and the doors locked. When the mailman dropped the mail through the slot, she had an anxiety attack. She lived on tranquilizers and tried to hold herself together to care for her twelve-year-old son and three-year-old daughter.

She was not able to work. If she managed to get to the grocery store, she imagined she saw the man and ran out without her groceries. She tried to attend church, but she could never get far without a great deal of medication. Her son was trying to help take care of his mother and little sister.

Vicki was right. Donna certainly needed inner healing. I knew from praying with Vietnam veterans and women who had been raped that inner healing was truly the best answer for post-traumatic stress, from which Donna obviously was suffering. Inner healing prayer does not erase or change the memory but transforms the effects of that memory in our lives to set us free.

I asked if it would be all right to go back to the memory of the robbery and invite Jesus to come into it. She said, "Yes, that's why I'm here."

After praying for the presence and power of the Holy Spirit and binding the enemy from interfering, I asked Donna to close her eyes while we prayed. "Donna," I said, "just in the quietness of this room, can you picture this memory?"

"Oh, yes," she said sorrowfully, "I see it every day. It has haunted me for two years! I feel his hand clutching my throat. I feel the cold metal of the gun against my temple. I can smell the man right now as I see this memory."

I opened my eyes and saw the anguish on her beautiful face. I knew in my heart how much the Lord loved her, and how He longed to release her from this prison.

I prayed: "Lord Jesus, I know how much You love Donna and how much this horrible experience is traumatizing her entire life. We ask You, Lord, as Donna remembers and re-experiences this memory, that You will come into it. Show her where You were when this happened. We invite You, Lord Jesus, to come into this time and place."

At this time I was very quiet, just waiting on the Holy Spirit. After a while, I heard Donna exclaim, "He was there. He was there! That's why the man didn't kill me!" Opening my eyes, I saw a physical transformation taking place in Donna.

The pain on her face was leaving. Peace began to replace her sadness and tears of joy ran down her cheeks. A light seemed to emanate from her head and face, and the darkness I had seen earlier was lifting. I asked if she could share with me what was happening.

"Well," she began, "I saw the memory of the man holding me from behind and holding the gun against my head. While he was screaming obscenities into my ear, the door opened and Jesus came through it. As Jesus stood there looking at us, the man became terrified and ran out the door! I always wondered why he left so fast—all of a sudden. Now, I know."

I felt the Lord wanted to heal the painful memories from her experiences in the psychiatric unit as well, so I asked Donna if this would be all right. "Let's do it," she replied enthusiastically. I asked the Lord to show her the memories that He wanted to heal that day.

The memory that came to Donna's mind was how concerned she was about her children during her extended stay in the hospital. She saw a mental picture of the one pay phone on the psychiatric floor and how all the patients wanted to use it at the same time.

In the picture, the Lord showed her how one of the other patients regularly made everyone else get off the phone and stood guard while Donna talked to her children. She realized that God was saying to her, *See, I was there with you in the hospital, too.*

She laughed after sharing this with me and said, "Do you think that girl could have been an angel?"

"Maybe so," I replied. "Nothing would surprise me."

Before we ended our prayer session, I asked the Lord if there was anything else He wanted me to do with Donna this day. What I heard Him say took me by surprise. He directed me to pray with Donna to experience the release of the Holy Spirit in her life, saying it would bring her much peace.

I asked Donna what she knew about the empowerment of the Holy Spirit. She said she knew a little about it because when she was able to go, she attended a church where some of the people operated in some of the gifts of the Spirit, meaning they prayed for healing, spoke in tongues, prophesied and used other gifts (see 1 Corinthians 12:1–11, 27–31).

I asked if she had ever experienced any of these gifts personally, and she said no. I smiled at her next comment because it is so typical of many Christians: "I thought the power of the Holy Spirit and its gifts were something God gave to you when He thought you were ready."

"Well, the Scriptures say it a little differently," I replied. "In the gospel of Luke we read that Jesus said, 'If you then, though you are evil, know how to give good gifts to your children, how much more will your Father in heaven give the Holy Spirit to those who ask him!'"

128

"You mean, all I have to do is ask for it?" she asked, surprised.

"Yes, that's what I'm saying," I said, thinking, *Oh, please, Lord, don't let me down here.*

"Okay, let's ask for it," Donna said with enthusiasm.

So I prayed something like this: "Lord, Your Scripture says all we need to do is ask for the release of the Holy Spirit in our lives. You know how much Donna has been through, and she needs the power of the Holy Spirit in her life. We are asking You today, Lord, to release this power in Donna. Thank You, Lord, that You have been with us here today in such a powerful way."

After a short while, Donna began praising God, giving Him all glory and honor. I was praying softly both in English and in my prayer language.

All of a sudden, Donna began praying out loud in tongues, praising God intermittently with both her prayer language and English. What a beautiful experience this was! It was truly a holy moment, to be so present in the fullness of God's Spirit. I am not even aware of how long we stayed in this beautiful place of praise and worship.

Before Donna left I suggested she look in the mirror on my office wall. She stood transfixed at the bright, joyful face staring back at her.

"Oh!" she exclaimed. "I really am different!" I knew then that this had truly been a divine appointment and that Donna's life would never be the same.

After Donna left, our receptionist came up to me and inquired, "Was that the same girl who went into your office two hours ago? She looks totally different!"

With pure delight I said, "Well, yes and no." God is truly an awesome God!

I spoke to Donna several weeks later and she said when she went back to her psychiatrist for her weekly appointment, he asked, "What happened to you?" And she replied, "I'm going to tell you about Jesus, and you're going to listen!"

The last I heard from Donna, she was off all anti-anxiety medication, no longer in psychiatric treatment, attending church regularly and experiencing tremendous peace. She was also beginning to work part-time.

Please note that, as we will see below, healing does not always happen this fast. It takes courage to face painful memories and many times the hurts have built for years. Do not be discouraged if progress seems slow. Jesus wants to heal and will work with you as long as it takes. Our healing will always be a work in process. The Holy Spirit is a true gentleman, allowing us to move at a comfortable pace.

Emotional Healing from Trauma Wounds

Donna's story is a classic example of a trauma wound, the emotional or mental abuse inflicted upon us by other people. Trauma wounds from pain and suffering inflicted over a prolonged period of time can cause horrific damage to our spirits. Satan can use these wounds to wreak havoc in our lives. You may be thinking that this is not fair. Satan never plays fair. He sees these wounds as prime opportunities to cause us further pain.

For example, I have ministered to many men and women who have been sexually abused and victims of incest. After a period of time, spirits of lust or hatred or rage can begin to oppress a person. In such instances, Satan uses trauma wounds as starting points for a wealth of other oppressive areas that he uses to break us down.

Such was the case with Theresa. Theresa was a victim of incest by her father and later by her brother for a period of years. As a result of this abuse, the enemy got a foothold in Theresa's life. Severe hatred, especially of men, lodged in her heart.

Along with this hatred, Theresa believed the lie that all men are bad and not to be trusted. She dated little, became extremely overweight and never allowed herself to entertain the idea of marriage or having children. Dealing with male authority figures at work and having a male landlord created additional stress for Theresa. Her overeating became compulsive.

A great deal of prayer for emotional healing was necessary before Theresa could forgive her father and brother and begin seeing God as a loving, nurturing parent. Inviting the Lord into her memories of abuse, letting the Lord reveal the lies from the enemy that she had believed, and praying for the Holy Spirit to guide her eating habits were key in Theresa's recovery.

Trauma wounds often seem to have the enemy's hand of hatred and spite behind them.

A young man I know went away to college and was having a difficult time fitting in with the other male students in his dormitory. A group of boys decided to amuse themselves at his expense. They decided to drink until they became sick and then to vomit into plastic bags. They continued with this until they had a large volume and planned their attack for a night when he was studying in the library. When the young man returned, he found that they had emptied their bags throughout his room, desecrating his clothes, furniture, typewriter and books. He was never the same after this.

I have heard many stories of this type of abuse from the "fat kids" or "tall and skinny kids" or the "poor kids" who wore the same clothes each day because that was all they had. And what about the trauma and abuse inflicted on boys who are particularly small or feminine, not good at sports, but great in drama, music and art? Some of them spend their entire lives looking for healthy male attention, needing and desiring to fit in. Many never find it.

But Jesus can bring love, peace and comfort to the trauma memories and any area in need of emotional healing. He is all-powerful and He is not bound by time or space. Through the power of the Holy Spirit, He is able to reach back and touch those places of darkness so that in the future, the memory is full of His peace and His presence. Jesus truly has come to "bind up the brokenhearted and set the captives free."

131

How to Pray for Emotional Healing

The following is an abbreviated checklist of questions to help you discern if inner healing might be helpful for you or someone you love:

1. Were you greatly embarrassed when you were a child or young adult?
2. Do you have unreasonable fears?
3. Do you often find that your reaction to something said or done is out of proportion to whatever the stimulus was?
4. Do you have a recurring memory of a past hurt? Does it still trouble you to think about it?
5. Are there people you cannot forgive? Do you have trouble asking someone else to forgive you?
6. Do you have overwhelming feelings of guilt?
7. Do you find it nearly impossible to admit making a mistake? Do you usually look for someone else to blame for what goes wrong in your life?
8. Do you have a nearly continuous feeling of anger? Are you usually critical in your remarks or thoughts about others?
9. Do you suffer physical or mental exhaustion from wrestling with inner problems?
10. Were you an adult before you ever felt loved by another person?
11. Do you often compare yourself with others and end up feeling inadequate and discouraged?
12. Do you have a constant need for physical affection, or do you not like to be touched at all?
13. Do you have a deep sense of insecurity, feeling unloved or disapproved of?
14. Is it hard for you to believe that God loves you or approves of you?
15. Do you find it difficult to give and receive love?

If you answered yes to any of these questions, I encourage you to allow the Lord to walk back into these places with you and begin healing the memories. Again, remember: The Lord Jesus is not bound by time or space.

An important aspect of any healing prayer is to bind off the enemy and pray for the release of the Holy Spirit. This is especially vital when praying for inner healing for yourself or someone you love. Remember that the enemy has held the person in bondage with these memories, creating years of shame, guilt, fear and rejection. He does not want to let the person go. Bind off all interference of the enemy. Pray for the power of the Holy Spirit.

Your prayer may go something like this:

In the name of Jesus Christ, with the authority given to me as a Christian, I bind all interference or disruption of this prayer session. By the blood and the power of the cross, I bind all enemies of Christ.

Come, Holy Spirit. Cleanse and purify this room from anything not of You. Make this room a holy place, Lord, with the power of Your Spirit and Your love present.

Give us wisdom, knowledge and discernment as we pray in the areas needing inner healing. Give us courage and trust in You, Lord, as You reveal specific memories. We thank You and praise You in Jesus' holy, precious name. Amen.

Following is a sample prayer to use when beginning to pray for emotional, or inner, healing. If you are praying for yourself, insert your own name in the appropriate places. It is perfectly all right to experience emotional healing alone with God. I have received healing of the memories in a group setting, with a small prayer team and alone during my quiet time.

Lord Jesus, I thank You for [name]. I thank You for the opportunity to be here today, gathering together in Your name. Lord, I know that [name] is Your child and that You know everything

133

there is to know about [name]. Thank You for loving [name] so much. I thank You that You have brought [name] to this place today to receive Your healing in specific areas of [her/his/my] life. Lord, I ask that by the power of Your Holy Spirit, You show [name] the first memory You want to heal today.

Wait quietly. After the Lord brings to mind the memory, invite the Lord into the memory: "Lord, I thank You for bringing this memory to mind. I know, Lord, that You showed it for a reason and that You want to heal this place of hurt. Lord, I invite You to come into this memory with Your love and holy presence. Come, Lord Jesus, with Your healing power." Wait in silence.

Caution: When praying for another person, it is important *not* to dictate what the Lord does in this memory. Dictating the Lord's involvement is called "guided imagery" and is the reason inner healing has been criticized by some as being New Age. The Lord taught me long ago that my job as a prayer minister is only to invite Him into the memory. He does all the rest.

Everyone sees, feels and experiences the Lord in different ways. The Lord is able to come into a memory and heal it in an especially individualized manner for each person. Let the Holy Spirit work.

It is also important to recognize that an extremely cerebral person may find it difficult to experience the mental pictures as described above. The Lord has taught me in these circumstances to ask the person, "What do you *think* Jesus would do in the healing of this memory?"

After the healing of the first memory, proceed in the same manner with additional memories. Ask the Holy Spirit as you go along how much inner healing He wants to accomplish in this session. After years of prayer ministry experience, I have seen the majority of people with whom I have prayed receive this type of healing in one or more of the following ways:

1. They feel deep peace come over them and into the memory.
2. They see light or a brightness that fills the memory.
3. They can actually see the Lord Jesus come into the memory.
4. They hear the Lord's voice actually speak to them in their minds or spirits.

Doctors, medication and therapy can help people cope with the pain of trauma, depression and post-traumatic stress. But what can truly change a person from the inside out is the power of the Holy Spirit through emotional, or inner, healing. When God's healing power reaches into those memories and the presence of the Lord Jesus comes into that place of sadness, negativity or despair, a transformation takes place. It is impossible for us to alter the past and its effects on us, but through the power of God the Holy Spirit, we can remove the crippling effects of sin inflicted on our lives.

EIGHT

HEALING FOR THE CONCEPTION-TO-BIRTH EXPERIENCE

For you created my inmost being; you knit me together in my mother's womb. I praise you because I am fearfully and wonderfully made; your works are wonderful, I know that full well. My frame was not hidden from you when I was made in the secret place. When I was woven together in the depths of the earth, your eyes saw my unformed body. All the days ordained for me were written in your book before one of them came to be.

PSALM 139:13–16

"Before I formed you in the womb I knew you, before you were born I set you apart."

JEREMIAH 1:5

We have seen one of the most wonderful aspects of God at work: the fact that He is not limited by time or space. With

137

His wonderful power, mercy and grace, He is able to reach back and heal the memories or hurts from the past. This means every bit of our pasts, including the days and months we spent in the womb.

It is a sad but true fact that some people experience physical and emotional damage from the time of conception, during their months in utero. This is something of a mystery, but children in the womb are aware of much more than we might realize. In addition, they are utterly defenseless as they hear and feel anything frightening that is going on in the world around them.

The good news is that emotional, or inner, healing prayer can actually heal and restore those damaged places as well. In fact, praying for healing from conception to birth is one of the most powerful forms of emotional healing.

A person can need healing prayer about the in utero experience for a variety of emotions they suffered. One of the first is rejection, particularly if the person was not conceived under the sanctity of a godly marriage. Perhaps the parents were not married to one another or the child was conceived in lust, rape, fornication or adultery. Perhaps the child was conceived while a parent was under the influence of drugs or alcohol.

Through the years, I have ministered to many adults whose parents had to get married because the woman was pregnant. Because of the legalization of abortion and the acceptance of single parenting, this is not as common as it was in years past. Many people have stated to me that they know without a doubt if abortion had been legal when their parents conceived them, they would never have been born.

Matt's parents married because his mother was pregnant with him and because of this Matt's father missed attending college on a football scholarship. Matt's mother felt tremendous hate and resentment toward this baby, demonstrating her feelings freely. For years, Matt suffered with bedwetting, and many of his childhood memories were of awakening in the middle of the night when his mother came in and checked the sheets. When the bed was wet, he was beaten as his mother screamed vile criticisms.

As Matt reached his teenage years, she yelled continually, "You ruined my life!" As a result of this emotional and physical abuse, Matt suffered from low self-esteem and rejection. I remember seeing him at a spiritual retreat one Sunday, which happened to be Mother's Day. After he wished me a happy Mother's Day, I asked if he would be seeing his mother. He responded, "She'll have a great Mother's Day. Since I'm out of town, she won't have to see me!"

Knowing this was true, I felt tremendous sadness—not only for Matt but also for his mother who was not able to love and enjoy the special gift God had given her in her son. In Matt's emotional healing, it was important to begin by praying from conception to birth, where his rejection began. We spent a great deal of time with Matt praying that God would heal the emotional scars he received while in his mother's womb.

Matt began to realize that he was created by God, that the Lord's hand was on his life and that God had a plan and purpose for him. We then prayed for emotional healing and invited the Lord into his hurtful memories. This emotional healing gradually brought about new confidence in Matt. He began advancing into leadership positions. He also met a wonderful young lady at church who, he discovered, loved him unconditionally. They have been happily married for ten years.

Fear is another emotion that many people experience before they are born, sometimes even when they truly are wanted by both parents. Let's take, for example, a mother who has tried for years to conceive and carry a child to full term. Throughout her marriage she has experienced a number of miscarriages, each occurring at varying times in the first eight weeks of pregnancy.

Finally, she has almost made it through the first trimester. What are the primary feelings that are transferred to this baby from the mother? Fear and anxiety! This mother has wanted a child desperately, longing and praying for a successful pregnancy. Both she and her husband are afraid even to hope that she will carry this child to full term.

This type of prenatal experience can have lasting effects upon a child. And Satan can use this opportunity to instill fear in a child, fear that can affect the child's entire life.

If fear is also a generational issue for this person, you can understand how he or she might be bound by all types of fear: fear of rejection, fear of abandonment, fear of the future, fear of the unknown and so on.

A beautiful young woman named Karen came for prayer with the presenting problem of fear. Adopted as a baby, Karen already had worked through many of her rejection and abandonment issues. As a committed Christian and believer in healing prayer, Karen knew the Lord could help with this continual fear as well.

Karen said she could never remember a time when she did not experience fear on some level, which led me to believe it began in utero. I also asked her a question that often helps me determine whether or not we are dealing with a spirit of fear sent from the enemy. I inquired, "Karen, when you experience this fear—does it have a hold on you or do you have a hold on it?"

"It has a hold on me! It is a gut-wrenching fear. My heart pounds and I am unable to think rationally or convince myself there is nothing to be afraid of. The fear just kind of takes over."

"We know you were adopted," I said, "but is there anything else you know about your birth parents, anything that would explain this tremendous fear you experience?"

"As a matter of fact," she replied, "I know a great deal about my birth parents. I met my birth mother several years ago and she gave me helpful information about my family history and background. I have met a number of my relatives.

"My birth parents were married to each other and my mother was a teenager. My father was a drug user at this time, using acid and marijuana, and moving to heroin after I was born. In fact, my biological father went to prison for drug dealing as did my biological brother. My father was a habitual offender charged with battery.

"My father was very abusive, especially to my mother, giving her black eyes and broken bones. He would go off on binges and come home and beat her. While she was pregnant with me, my father physically abused her while strung out on drugs. Because I was so close in age to my brother, both parents decided to give me up for adoption."

After hearing this story, I felt certain that the fear began in utero and that we needed to pray for the Lord to reveal His presence during Karen's time in the womb. As we prayed, inviting Jesus to enter into this time of pain and terror, Karen began to cry uncontrollably. After a period of loud wailing, tremendous peace began to settle upon her.

Describing the experience later, Karen said, "I was just filled with peace and love. It was as though God came in and healed the fear that was put into me as a little baby, a little fetus, in the womb."

Karen experienced an immediate change in her attitude. Working as a waitress while attending college, she was always shy and timid around her customers, never looking them in the eye. The very afternoon of her healing, while working, she experienced a freedom and confidence she had never known.

She told me later, "I just looked customers in the eye and was extremely confident, and I felt happy and secure," she reported. "It was unreal what God did because Satan had used that fear to chain me and bind me and put it around me like some type of stronghold from the time I was a baby. It was there my whole life! Then when God came and healed me and delivered me of that fear, it was incredible—the confidence and peace and stability and security that came after that. It was so awesome. God is so awesome!"

Karen's healing of fear was a key turning point in her spiritual and emotional life. She experienced no fear while carrying her daughter, Alyssa, having a wonderful pregnancy and delivery. She presently teaches in an inner-city school. With students towering over her, she is able to control her class with quiet dignity. Fear, once her constant companion, is now replaced with peace and confidence.

A baby in utero can experience other emotions that are not life-giving as well. Imagine a mother who is the caregiver for a dying parent or a terminally ill child or perhaps someone whose husband dies during the pregnancy. Think of the pain, grief and sorrow involved in this type of tremendous loss.

It also can be difficult on the baby in utero when the birth mother is physically ill or suffers some type of accident or injury during her pregnancy. My daughter-in-law, Vicki, had two automobile accidents while carrying her son, Andrew. One was a little fender bender but the other was more serious. She prayed immediately after the accidents, and we all prayed for both Vicki and her unborn child for healing of the memories of the accidents and for peace.

Many people need healing prayer back to the time of delivery. I prayed with a woman named Lucille who was afraid of having a committed relationship that might lead to marriage. Asking the Lord to reveal the root of this fear brought out in the open her true fear: She was not so much afraid of marriage but of the thought that her husband might want children. She was terrified at the thought of being pregnant and especially of the whole delivery process.

When asked what her mother's pregnancy had been like she responded, "It wasn't the pregnancy that was so bad but the delivery. I was born during a horrible hurricane in Mississippi. My mother was barricaded in the house and I guess the fear and anxiety of the storm caused her to go into early labor.

"I entered this world during a violent storm, with wind and rain snapping the trees from their roots around my house. With the ferociousness of the wind, the roof was ripped off. The beams of the house came crashing down around us. My aunt was killed during this storm, right there in the house, and other family members also were injured."

In prayer, we asked Jesus to reveal His presence to Lucille during this hurricane and the time of her delivery. Able to see Jesus there, kneeling beside her mother, lovingly holding her hand, Lucille said she experienced tremendous peace that flowed into her as a little baby still nestled inside her mother's womb. After a while she saw herself being born, and the Lord was there, ready to receive her with loving arms. She felt tremendous joy, love and protection.

This healing brought Lucille to a new place in her relationship with Jesus. Within a year, she married a wonderful man and experienced excitement about the prospect of having children. When she became pregnant, she called to let me know that she felt absolutely wonderful and asked me to pray for her and the health of the baby. Now the mother of two beautiful children, she enjoyed both her pregnancies and had peaceful, normal deliveries.

Another example of hurtful emotions for a child in the womb is when the parents want a child of one sex and give birth to a child of the other sex. This is a very common occurrence. Every person reading this right now has an idea of whether or not you were a disappointment to your parents because of your sex. Perhaps you were told by a parent or family member or overheard someone talking about it.

Feelings of confusion abound in a person who thinks that he or she is a disappointment. A child in the womb actually knows if he or she is wanted and can be afraid of coming into the world. Who would want to come into a place knowing he is not wanted?

In addition to praying through the birth experience with inner healing prayers, God has shown me another type of help. When a person struggles with not wanting to be born, I suggest that he begin praying every day:

Lord Jesus, help me to want to be born. Help me to want to come forth and embrace life. Help me to choose life and want to come into Your world. Lord, grant me Your peace.

A close friend of mine named Elizabeth has a powerful teaching and testimony about the importance of praying from conception to birth:

A number of years ago, I heard a talk on the importance of praying for an unborn child. Listening to the talk, I heard the speaker mention the word *ambivalence.* When he said the word *ambivalence,* I heard the Lord say, *Elizabeth, that's the way it was with you. On the one hand, your parents were very excited about your coming, but on the other hand, it was very bad timing.*

When He said that, two things became very clear to me. First, it explained why I always felt that I was imposing on people. I felt, for instance, that when I went into a room I needed to apologize for being there. I thought that I was just an intrusion somehow in people's lives.

Second, it made me understand and know that I was conceived before my parents were married, and that was something that had never occurred to me. I am the oldest of seven children, and it made a lot of sense to me what the Lord had said.

I later found out, after speaking to my mother about this a number of years later, that the bad timing did not just have to do with the fact that they conceived me before they were married. It also had to do with the fact that my dad had been accepted at a military academy: Only single men were allowed to attend.

It was something my dad had worked very hard to achieve, and another officer even offered to lie and say that he did not have a family so that he could go. But he said no, that he had a responsibility and that he needed to take care of my mother and me. So he didn't go and that was also part of the bad timing.

All of this was a confirmation, that what I heard from the Lord was right. But I think the most important thing was that the family secret and shame were exposed. I loved them for the fact that they cared enough about me to have me and raise me. It showed me a demonstration of their love, so I think it was very good for my mother and me finally to talk about it.

It also demonstrated my dad's sense of commitment to me, and to our family, and to my mom.

After this revelation, Elizabeth shared her story with me and asked if we could pray together. During our prayer time, we asked the Lord to heal any areas in Elizabeth's memory about her conception, her time in utero or her parent's marriage. Elizabeth told me what transpired in that prayer:

> The one thing I did know about my birth experience was that my father wasn't there. He was trying to get to the hospital. That was the only clear thing I knew, other than what the Lord had just shown me. And when you prayed for me, you prayed first for any pattern of illegitimacy to be broken that may have come down through the generations. You placed the cross and blood of Jesus between me and my parents and the generations before them. You prayed that I would feel a sense of belonging and knowing the Lord wanted me.
>
> The thing I remember most about the prayer was the birth experience. I could see clearly my mother and the doctor getting ready to deliver me, and as you prayed, I was aware of the Lord standing next to the doctor. The Lord was standing there with His hands folded in excitement, like a little child would be—just so excited! I could hear the Lord say, "I am so glad you're here."
>
> I felt so much joy and excitement about the Lord's anticipation that I was coming, and when I saw how happy He was that I was there, it made me excited to be there. The next thing I remember is being in the room with my mother. My mother was holding me, and my father had arrived by that time, and we were all together.
>
> There was a hallway near the room we were in, and my grandmother was coming down that hallway. I could feel this strong sense of embarrassment, shame and annoyance that this was bad timing.
>
> She was not happy or joyous or excited about me. She was embarrassed that my parents had to get married. And as she

145

moved toward the room I was in, I could feel that sense of being unhappy and embarrassed.

The next thing I remember is that the Lord enveloped me with peace. I sensed that what was happening with my grand-mother really had nothing to do with me. She felt shame and that was *her* issue. But it did not take away from the Lord wanting me and expecting me with great anticipation and joy, and my parents wanting me to be there. So, even though I sensed the feelings of my grandmother, I did not take them in. I felt free from that connection. I was able to recognize that my grandmother had issues that she herself was trying to deal with, but I wasn't responsible. I no longer felt that I was an imposition on people. I knew that my place in this life was blessed by the Lord, and everything was okay. I didn't feel that sense of shame anymore.

Through the power of the Holy Spirit, God can reveal things to our hearts, as He did for Elizabeth. With His mighty power He can reach back into areas of woundedness of which we are not even aware. The important thing is to invite Him into those places and be willing to receive His healing.

A question often asked is how to pray for a person who is adopted. Often, there is concern about a person's lack of infor-mation about his or her conception or time in utero. Another beautiful thing about God, our Creator, is that He *knows* all there is to know about us. Recall the words from Jeremiah above: "Before I formed you in the womb I knew you, before you were born I set you apart." And look at the words of David: "From my mother's womb you have been my God" (Psalm 22:10).

Adopted persons often know whether the birth parents were married or have any predisposition to genetic illnesses. Many times the adoptive parents have shared some additional general information with them.

In prayer, proceed with the information you *do* have and rely on the Holy Spirit to fill in the blanks. The important thing is that you open yourself to this powerful form of inner healing and allow yourself to experience a new closeness with

God. God's healing hand can indeed reach back into our pasts, even before we were born, filling us with love, peace and the assurance of our belonging to Him, our Creator.

> Yet you brought me out of the womb; you made me trust in you even at my mother's breast. From birth I was cast upon you; from my mother's womb you have been my God.
>
> PSALM 22:9–10

How to Pray for Healing of the Conception-to-Birth Experience for Yourself

1. Think over everything you know about your birth experience. Did you come at a good time in your parents' lives? Were there previous miscarriages or abortions? Was there difficulty in the pregnancy or birth itself? Try to remember all stories you have heard from your parents, relatives or family friends. Invite Jesus into the moment of your conception.

2. Remember that before you were formed in your mother's womb, God knew you. He created you. His one purpose is for you to have a loving relationship with Him forever. God is your first and real parent, and He placed you in an earthly family.

3. Pray for release from genetic problems in your family. These would include such things as arthritis, cancer, diabetes, heart trouble, high blood pressure, manic depression and other mental disorders. Cut yourself free from generational bondage, such as alcoholism, incest or occult involvement.

4. Pray for God to fill your mother's womb with the power of the Holy Spirit, so that you may live and move and have your being in God. Let the Holy Spirit be the buffer between any negative thoughts, emotions or words of your mother or father.

147

5. Ask God to reassure you that He wanted and planned for you to be male or female. You were created by God. He had a plan and purpose for your life.
6. Open yourself to receive all the gifts, talents and tools God has designed especially for you.
7. Recognize that you were created with God's special love and uniqueness. There is not another person in the world like you. Pray for God to fill you with the knowledge of His presence, His safety and His peace as you grow and develop in the womb.
8. While praying about the delivery, get in touch with what you are feeling: fear, anxiety, excitement? Do you believe you wanted to be born? Do you perceive the world as unsafe, or do you want to come forth and experience life? Be very still and quiet, asking Jesus to help you choose life.
9. Can you see or feel the Lord? It may be through a bright light or a feeling of peace. Allow time for Jesus to receive you into His hands so the first touch you feel is His touch of strength, gentleness, warmth, security and safety. Give yourself ten to fifteen minutes of quiet time so that you might see or feel the Lord's presence. Let Jesus' face be the first face you ever see, and His voice the first you ever hear.

How to Pray for Healing of the Conception-to-Birth Experience for Another Person

1. Inquire respectfully about the person's birth process. Did he come at a good time in his parents' lives? Were there previous miscarriages or abortions? Was there difficulty in the pregnancy or birth itself? Through prayer, invite Jesus into the moment of conception.
2. Impress upon the person that before he was formed in his mother's womb, God knew him. He created this per-

son. His one purpose is for the person to have a loving relationship with Him forever. God is the first and real parent, and He placed this person in an earthly family.

3. Pray for release from genetic problems. Cut him free from generational bondage, such as alcoholism, mental instability, occult involvement, etc.

4. Pray for the womb to be filled with the power of the Holy Spirit so that the baby lives, moves and has his being in God. Let the Holy Spirit be the buffer between any negative thoughts, emotions or words of the mother or father.

5. Ask God to reassure the person that He wanted and planned for a male or female child.

6. Ask God to place within the person all the gifts, talents and tools that he will need to become the person God created.

7. Reassure the person of God's love and his uniqueness. Pray for God's presence, safety and peace as the child grows and develops.

8. When you reach the point of praying for the delivery, ask what the person is feeling: fear, anxiety, excitement? Many times, people never wanted to be born. They perceived the world as unsafe and never wanted to come forth. Ask if he is able to let Jesus help him choose life.

9. Ask gently if the person can see or feel the Lord. It may be through a bright light or a feeling of peace. Allow time for Jesus to receive him into His hands so the first touch the person ever feels is His touch of strength, gentleness, warmth, security and safety.

Allow ten or fifteen minutes of quiet time so that the person might see or feel Jesus' presence. Pray that Jesus' face will be the first face he ever sees, and that Jesus' voice will be the first voice he ever hears.

NINE

HEALING
OF OCCULT EXPERIENCES

Occult involvement is one of the enemy's favorite weapons to bring people into spiritual confusion. The occult, meaning "secret" or "hidden," is Satan's world of the spirit. It is dangerous because it appeals to our spiritual hunger, which is our innate desire to find and to know our Creator, but it actually separates us from Him.

The Bible teaches us that this enemy, Satan, is an angel who chose to rebel (Revelation 12:7–9). His free will, given to him by God, is *good,* but his choice to use it in rebellion is what brought *evil.* He has been cast out of heaven onto the earth, and God allows him to appeal to our own capacity for rebellion, our ego-side. The earth is his occupied territory. Jesus referred to him as the prince of this world (see John 14:30).

He stands as an alternative to choosing to love God. He is very clever, so he never asks us outright to follow him. Rather, he says in a subtle way, "Don't let anyone tell you what to do. Do your own thing. Look out for number one." He knows that if he can appeal to our rebellious nature, we are never going to obey God.

Satan would prefer to have us believe he is not real—that all the evil we encounter comes out of our own nature, or from other people, or that God put it here to make our lives difficult. He would love for us to blame God for all the trouble we experience and for the heartache we see in our world. If he is unable to convince us that he does not exist, he tries another tactic. This story skillfully illustrates this point.

One day Satan summoned one of his chief demons for a report and asked the following question: "How do you believe that we can best destroy mankind?"

The demon answered, "We can tell them there is no God."

"That will never work," replied Satan. "Look at the earth, the moon, the stars. Look at the creation. They know that God exists."

"Okay," the demon replied. "Let's tell them that you don't exist."

"No, no, that won't work either. They know I exist," replied Satan. "They can see the death and destruction around them. They can see famines, wars, broken families, child abuse. They know I exist."

"Okay," said the demon. "Let's tell them they have plenty of time."

Smiling his evil smile, Satan replied, "Aha—now that will work!"

Many times I have heard people say, "I'll get right with God one of these days. Right now I just want to do my own thing and put God on the back burner. After all, I might have to give up something. God might not like some of my behavior." So they worship other gods—gods like money, power and control. This is where occult practices come into play. Every individual I have ever known who became heavily involved in occult practices was trying to gain power and control in some area of his or her life.

Occult involvement is seeking to gain knowledge or power from a source other than God. Look at the definitions of the following occult words:

152

divination—an act of foretelling the future, assuming the help of unseen powers

enchant—to use magic words or charms to place someone under a spell

witch—one thought to have supernatural powers obtained through a contract with Satan

medium—one supposedly having access to supernatural agencies and knowledge or power derived from them

wizard—a sorcerer, one possessed of magic influence

necromancer—one who claims to reveal the future by communication with the dead

Each of these terms has two things in common. The first is the expectancy of having control and power in one's own life or in the life of another. Second, they are all an abomination to God.

Let no one be found among you who . . . practices divination or sorcery, interprets omens, engages in witchcraft, or casts spells, or who is a medium or spiritist [some translations say "wizard"] or who consults the dead. Anyone who does these things is detestable to the LORD.

DEUTERONOMY 18:10–12

When we open ourselves up to occult practices, we violate the first Commandment, "You shall have no other gods before me" (Exodus 20:3), and Jesus' commandment, a quote from Deuteronomy, to "Love the Lord your God with all your heart and with all your soul and with all your mind and with all your strength" (Mark 12:30; see also Deuteronomy 6:5; Matthew 22:37; Luke 10:27). The Bible is clear about God's hatred of the occult.

We need to remember that *all* occult involvement brings spiritual confusion. This confusion begins when we recognize that there are other spiritual forces besides God, and when we use them, attempt to consult them or are preoccupied with staying "on their good side." I heard a story that is a sad commentary on this deadly preoccupation. A dying man, asked by the priest if he renounced Satan and all of his ways, answered, "Now, Father, in my precarious state I would rather not make any more enemies than I have to."

Evelyn, an attractive, mature woman, came for ministry with the presenting problem of depression. Her Christian psychiatrist suggested she might be helped by receiving prayer ministry, especially for emotional healing. Evelyn especially was grieving the loss of her twin sister, whom she had lovingly nursed for two years before her death.

Evelyn and her sister, Elaine, were not only twins but best friends. When they were little girls, sickness and disaster plagued their family, and the children had to be separated from their parents. Together, Evelyn and Elaine went to live with an aunt and uncle and other relatives, not seeing the rest of their immediate family for a long time. This forged an even deeper bond than they already experienced as identical twins.

When Elaine died of cancer, Evelyn was inconsolable and despondent. She began wondering if she could still communicate with her sister. She read books about seances and channeling, a form of contacting the dead. This is what Whoopi Goldberg's character was doing in the movie *Ghost,* and although this popular movie made channeling seem comical and even fun, it is a very real and extremely dangerous occult practice. The more deeply Evelyn moved into these occult practices, the more confused and depressed she became.

Eventually, Evelyn was unable to pray, read her Bible or attend church. She was experiencing the spiritual confusion that comes with occult involvement. As she moved deeper into depression and grief, her husband and children were becoming even more alarmed. When her doctor suggested she come for prayer ministry and she agreed, her family was encouraged.

When Evelyn came for ministry, we spent a great deal of time praying about the loss of her sister, asking God to fill the loneliness. She expressed the difficulty she had when trying to pray and read the Scriptures in her home. From experience, I knew to ask about occult practices, such as books on the subject, Ouija boards, fortune-tellers, seances.

Evelyn was totally surprised when I informed her these practices went against God's Word and would cause spiritual confusion. Like so many others, she was unaware these things were dangerous and hazardous to her spiritual health. The pastor of her church had never mentioned the danger of occult practices.

Evelyn repented and renounced her involvement. She also discarded any books and materials that were offensive to God.

Immediately, Evelyn began to improve. She started to pray again, read the Scriptures and retain biblical truth. She started attending church regularly. The depression began to lift as she felt connected to her Lord once again. And in this renewed connectedness, Evelyn experienced peace about the death of her precious sister, knowing that they would be reunited in God's Kingdom.

As we learn from Evelyn's story, it is important to recognize that the wrong things we do in innocence and ignorance hurt just as much as the things we do deliberately. Satan has set occult traps throughout our world into which he hopes we will fall. God's way of healing us through confession, renouncement and forgiveness works not only for our sins but for our errors and our ignorance as well. It is vitally important to confess and receive forgiveness for our occult involvement, whether it was done in sin, error or ignorance.

I often hear people say, "Sure, I played with a Ouija board or had my palm read or attended a seance, but it didn't mean anything. I was just playing around."

Satan is a legalist. He is always looking for an entry point into our lives. And if you open a spiritual door for him, he has the right to go through it. He wants some form of power in or over us and will take whatever he can get any way he can get it. Remember that Jesus said Satan comes to rob, to kill and to destroy (see John 10:10).

Satan is driven by one purpose: to separate us from the Lord. If he can play upon our spiritual hungers to trap us into some occult dead end, then his purpose is well-served. It is true that people can draw upon Satan's evil power as they delve into occult activities such as foretelling the future by palm reading, tarot cards and astrological charts. These activities become his trap both for the ones using them and the ones they entice.

Occult involvement is only one of the avenues that our enemy, Satan, uses as a point of entry into our lives. He uses three other methods previously mentioned in earlier chapters. These include habitual sin, generational curses and trauma wounds. All three can be closely related to occult influences. Regarding generational curses, remember that the occult can influence our lives through our ancestors, even if we have never taken part in occult practices ourselves.

After having firsthand experience with the enemy, my father-in-law, the late Rev. Frank Dearing, learned to recognize how Satan operated. He went on to use this knowledge to help hundreds of people through prayer ministry.

Father Frank developed an occult inventory sheet to help people in the renunciation of occult practices. An abbreviated version of this occult sheet is listed here for your use in pinpointing possible occult influences in your life.

The Occult Sheet

See Ephesians 4:27, 6:10–18; 1 Peter 5:8–9.

As you read through the following lists, ask the Holy Spirit to recall to your mind every involvement you have had. Keep in mind that many of these activities are clearly of the occult; others may not be as apparent. Please mark any and all activities, even if there is a question in your mind as to their occult nature, so that you are confident that you renounce all *possible* occult or demonic influence in your life.

It is not my purpose to teach about each and every one of these activities and why they are considered occult; I am simply offering a solid framework for occult renouncement. I took Father Frank's list and reworked it for years while I was director of prayer ministry at Christian Healing Ministries. I have based my information on the teachings of Christians who are considered experts in this area.

If you have any questions about specific activities listed here, please consult one of the books referenced in the Suggested Reading List at the end of this book.

Circle each area in which you have participated, whether or not it was "just for fun," out of curiosity or in earnest.

Soothsayers/Fortune-tellers

See Deuteronomy 18:9–16; Isaiah 2:6; Daniel 2:26–28; Acts 16:16.

1. Have you ever had your fortune told by tea leaves, palm reading, a crystal ball, a fortune-teller or any other means?
2. Have you ever read or followed horoscopes, or had a chart made for yourself to predict your future? Have you ever read any other type(s) of birth signs?

Necromancy, Spiritualism

See Leviticus 19:31, 20:6; 1 Samuel 28:7–11; 2 Kings 21:6; Isaiah 8:19–22.

3. Have you ever attended a seance or spiritualist meeting?
4. Do you believe in reincarnation? Have you ever had a reincarnation reading?
5. Have you ever played with a Ouija board, crystal ball, Dungeons & Dragons or other occult games?
6. Have you ever had a tarot card reading or practiced cartomancy (using playing cards for fortune-telling or other magical purposes)?

7. Have you ever played games of an occult nature, using ESP, telepathy, hypnotism, etc.?
8. Have you ever consulted a medium, spiritualist or numerologist? Have you ever acted as a medium? Have you ever practiced channeling?
9. Have you ever sought healing through magic spells or charms or through a spiritualist? Have you ever used a charm or amulet of any kind for protection or "good luck"? Are you superstitious?
10. Have you ever practiced table lifting, levitation of objects, pendulum swinging, lifting of bodies, automatic writing, astral travel or soul travel?

Occult Books, "Contact" Objects and Other Media

See Exodus 19:25–20:6; Deuteronomy 5:8–10, 7:25–26; 2 Kings 23:1–25; Psalm 97:7; Isaiah 42:17; 2 Corinthians 10:3–5.

11. Do you have anything in your home that was given to you by someone in the occult? Do you have anything in your home of an occult nature? Have you followed the writings of Edgar Cayce, Jean Dixon or a New Age author? Do you own or like to view demonic types of books or movies?

Sorcery or Magic

See 2 Kings 17:17, 21:6; Malachi 3:5; Acts 8:11, 13:4–12, 19:19–20.

12. Have you ever practiced sorcery or magic?
13. Have you ever practiced mind control over any person or animal, cast a magic spell or sought a psychic experience? Have you ever contacted a psychic in person or through a psychic hotline?

Sins of the Flesh, Sins of the Eyes

See Matthew 5:28; Romans 6:12–14, 8:13–14; 1 Corinthians 6:13, 18–20; Galatians 5:16–21; 1 Thessalonians 4:3–8; James 1:14–15; 1 Peter 2:11; 1 John 2:16.

14. Have you ever used LSD, marijuana, cocaine, crack-cocaine or any mind-expanding or mind-altering drugs? Have you ever abused prescription drugs? Have you ever had a problem with alcohol?
15. Have you ever exposed yourself to pornography in magazines, TV or stage shows, books, topless bars or X-rated movies?
16. Have you been involved in sexual deviation, homosexuality or lesbianism?
17. Have you ever had sexual relations with a person who was not your legal spouse? If possible, recall by name (first name or initial is sufficient).
18. Have you had an abortion? Have you fathered a child who was aborted? Have you been involved in abortion in any way (viewed/witnessed one, assisted in one, performed one, encouraged a friend to have one, had a botched abortion, etc.)?

Devil Worship

See 2 Chronicles 11:15; Psalm 106:37; 1 Corinthians 10:20–22; Revelation 9:20–21, 13:4.

19. Have you ever made a pact with Satan or been involved in or witnessed Satan worship or black magic?

Witchcraft

See 1 Samuel 15:23, 28:7; 2 Kings 9:22, 23:24; Isaiah 8:19, 19:3, 29:4; Micah 5:12.

20. Have you ever attended witchcraft or voodoo activities?

Death

See Exodus 20:13; Job 3:20–23; 1 Corinthians 6:19–20.

21. Have you ever planned or attempted to take your own life?
22. Have you ever planned or attempted to take someone else's life?

The Ministry of Authority

One of the important things Father Dearing passed on to me and others was the knowledge of our authority as Christians. Our authority comes from the power of Jesus, through His name and His blood.

Before Jesus sent His disciples out to work in ministry, He "gave them authority to drive out evil spirits and to heal every disease and sickness. . . . These twelve Jesus sent out with the following instructions: . . . 'Heal the sick, raise the dead, cleanse those who have leprosy, drive out demons'" (Matthew 10:1, 5, 8). He also said, "If you forgive anyone his sins, they are forgiven" (John 20:23).

This is the ministry of *authority,* His authority, passed on to His committed followers: "All authority in heaven and on earth has been given to me" (Matthew 28:18); "As the Father has sent me, I am sending you" (John 20:21).

Jesus overcame Satan in those forty days in the wilderness, and ultimately in His death and resurrection. He has authority over Satan and all evil spirits, and they know it. When He gives an order, they obey. As His followers, *we have His authority.* Our *authority* over evil comes from our *belonging* to the Lord Jesus and moving in His name.

Our power comes forth from the Holy Spirit moving in us and moving out from us to destroy the enemies of God. As we live day by day in the power of the Spirit, we find ourselves more and more able to recognize the occult traps of the enemy and to move in our authority.

The following is a prayer of authority, binding the enemy and praying for a release of the Holy Spirit. This is something I do each day, especially before I minister to another or speak or teach at a conference:

With the authority given to me as a Christian, I bind all enemies of Christ. I pray for a release of the power of the Holy Spirit in this place. Come, Lord Jesus. Guide and direct us in all Your ways. Amen.

Another prayer I often use specifically in the renunciation of occult involvement and the breaking of curses is also a prayer of authority. After going through the occult sheet, considering areas where Satan may have gained control in your life, and renouncing them all, I would encourage you to speak as follows:

Satan, I say to you in the name of Jesus, release me and my family from any hold you have had. I take back any territory I may have given you in the name of Jesus. I cancel any curse against me or any member of my family. I claim the protection of the blood of Jesus over my mind, body and spirit. I close the door on you, Satan—never to be opened again!

A nurse came for prayer after she was diagnosed with breast cancer. Betsy was the daughter of a minister, raised in a Christian home and married to a Christian pastor. At first glance, she did not seem a likely candidate for occult renouncement. After several visits, it became obvious that Betsy had rebelled during her college days and gone in search of power, finding it in occult forms. The following is Betsy's story.

161

Because I was so involved in Christian activities, I don't think Norma saw me as a likely candidate for dabbling in the occult when we first began meeting together. After all, my father was a minister and so is my husband. I had been in the church for most of my life.

During my late teens and early twenties, however, I drifted away from the church. I wanted very much to connect with something greater than myself. I believe today that many of my decisions and activities during this time were an attempt to find that something greater than myself. I had become disillusioned with the church.

I was raised by a very rigid and legalistic minister-father, and I believe that a significant reason I did not feel connected to God was because the God presented to me in my teens was a God of fire, brimstone and wrath. Today I don't blame my father for this. He only passed on to me the image of God that was presented to him when he was a child. I had experienced some major rejections in my life up to this point, and I believed I had been abandoned and rejected by God. Today I see that God never left me; it was I who had drifted away from God.

I look back today, and I see the subtle ways the enemy crept into my life. I remember using the Ouija board when I was about age thirteen. Over the next two years, I took part in seances and even led them, and I attended pajama parties where we lifted bodies. At age seventeen, I became very interested in ESP and the writings of Edgar Cayce and Jean Dixon. At age eighteen, I was introduced to self-hypnosis, which I practiced on and off for many years. I also hypnotized friends upon request.

It was also at this age that I had my fortune told with cards. In my early twenties, I was fascinated by the book *Helter Skelter* and the movie *The Exorcist*. When I was 21, I owned a voodoo doll necklace to which I had a definite attachment. I did throw it away after having it for about a year, however, because something inside of me felt it was evil.

Other events in my early twenties included a palm reading, which stimulated me to read books on the subject. For several years, I read people's palms and sometimes told them things about themselves I had no way of knowing. I remember telling one young man that at age sixteen he had gotten a girl pregnant, which was true. Another time I told a young woman that she had a rare blood disease, which she did. None of these things I knew, as I did not even know the people before I read their palms.

In my twenties I was suicidal, although I never attempted suicide. I have had suicidal ideations at several points in my life. I also smoked my share of pot, drank to excess, practiced yoga and was a regular reader of horoscopes.

I returned to the church at age 24 and married a minister at age 25. From age 25 through 35, I was at war with God, or so I thought. Not only did I feel that God had abandoned me, but I also felt that God often took my husband away from me to do God's work. This was a repeat of the way I felt growing up when my parents were often too busy doing God's work to give me the attention I needed and wanted.

I felt that God had caused these important people in my life to abandon me physically and emotionally. Through Christian counseling and my involvement with Twelve-Step programs, I have come to separate my pseudo-abandonment and rejection issues from God and have been able to see that these were issues I had with my father, mother and husband.

Through working the Twelve Steps, I have come to see my part in conflicts with people, as well as being able to see and be responsible for my character defects. I also have come to know personally the Higher Power whom I recognize as God. God was the something I had always looked for.

About six years ago, I became a registered nurse. The medical knowledge I have acquired has reinforced my belief that spiritual and emotional healing must go along with physical healing if a person is to advance toward wholeness. My diagnosis of breast cancer came at a time in my life when in many ways I was just beginning to feel alive. It was truly a shock.

When I began seeing Norma for prayer ministry, I felt desperate and determined to rid my body, soul and mind of anything that could set the stage for the cancer to return. The cancer was removed from my body through a mastectomy as well as treatment of chemotherapy. Emotional healing was achieved through healing of the memories, visualization of the Lord's presence, and the love and support of my Twelve-Step group and prayer partners.

When I look back over the events of my life, I know without a doubt that the wrong things I did in innocence and ignorance have hurt me as much as the things I did deliberately. I see how subtly evil entered my life over the years. It was necessary for me to do "housecleaning" of the things in my life that weren't of God. After going over the occult sheet with Norma, I went through my house and threw away every book, cassette tape, object—anything I felt could come between my Lord and me.

One tool to which Norma introduced me is the "Binding Prayer." I begin and end my days with this prayer. I use it during the day if I feel that spiritual warfare is going on in my life or in the lives of my loved ones. There have been times when my children have been in physical conflict and are yelling at each other, and I have gone into the closet and prayed this prayer. Within seconds, the house has become quiet.

On our recent vacation to the mountains, I did some serious praying for the binding of all enemies of Christ. This year was the first vacation we have ever had as a family without any arguments, harsh words or major conflicts between family members.

Today I am grateful to be alive, and I praise God for the healing that I have experienced, not only physically but spiritually and emotionally as well. God is good, and I proudly say, Jesus is the Lord over my life today.

A Prayer for Healing of Occult Influences

Most of us have been touched by the occult in some way and need to be cleansed and set free from the effects it has had in our lives. You may want to find some understanding Christian to join you in prayer so that as you confess these things to God, he or she can minister God's healing to you. "Therefore confess your sins to each other and pray for each other so that you may be healed" (James 5:16).

You may use something like the following:

Person: Lord, I confess that I have taken part in the following: *[name everything you circled in the occult sheet].* I see these now as sins and I ask Your forgiveness by the blood of Your cross.

Friend: In the name of Jesus, this is forgiven as if it had never been.

Person: Thank You, Lord, for this forgiveness. I renounce you, Satan, and everything you have had in me. I command you in Jesus' name to depart from me and trouble me no more.

Friend: I take the sword of the Spirit, the Word of God, and cut you free from every bondage to the occult world. I close the door between you and that world and seal it with the blood of Jesus and bar it with His cross.

Walk carefully in your healing, asking for the Lord's protection, staying close to His Word and His people.

TEN

CUTTING FREE FROM UNHOLY UNIONS AND UNHEALTHY RELATIONSHIPS

When I talk at conferences and retreats about the need to be cut free from unholy unions and unhealthy relationships, I am often met with a hushed and uncomfortable silence. Yet no one likes the prospect of maintaining a connection to past unhealthy relationships, especially if those relationships occurred before coming to know Jesus.

And the potential for ongoing hurt from these connections does not apply solely to the physical realm: Sexual activity brings about spiritual connections that can be deadly. This is why it is important to pray to be cut free spiritually and emotionally from anyone with whom you have been connected in an unhealthy manner. In order to walk in the fullness of God's healing, we must address the past in this way.

Let me show you what I mean.

Cutting Free from Sexual Relationships

When we join with a person physically, whether it is in fornication, adultery or homosexuality, we also join that person emotionally and spiritually. Paul states: "Do you not know that he who unites himself with a prostitute is one with her in body? For it is said, 'The two will become one flesh'" (1 Corinthians 6:16).

If we think in terms of being "connected" to all the people in the past with whom we have had intimate physical relationships, it is wrenching to contemplate. If we further consider that we are not only connected to these people, but also to everyone with whom they had sexual relations, and so on, and so on, it is almost incomprehensible. Do I have your attention?

There seems to be greater understanding of the physical ramifications of sexual unions since the AIDS epidemic. The very fact that the virus can be transmitted by sexual union and lie dormant for several years has brought this to our attention. Sexually active people have difficulty tracing where they became infected.

God created sex to be good and pure—to be a beautiful wedding gift to the couple joined in holy matrimony. God created the concept of marriage, and His plan for marriage is clear and specific: "For this reason a man will leave his father and mother and be united to his wife, and they will become one flesh" (Genesis 2:24). Sexual union, or oneness, between a husband and wife was created by God to be sanctified, to be holy.

This is why I believe the enemy, Satan, has spent so much time and energy trying to distort the beauty of sexual union and the whole concept of the Christian marriage. As we look around our world, we see his evil hand in so many areas of sexual distortion. Rape, incest, sexual abuse, fornication, adultery, homosexuality and lesbianism are all examples of how the enemy has twisted what God intended for a man and a woman in marriage.

In my particular Christian denomination, we speak of "the world, the flesh and the devil." I find that each of these is a major contributor to sexual immorality. They can lead to destructive patterns of behavior and trap a person in sin, shame and guilt, and away from the one true satisfying thing—a relationship with the Lord.

Christians must constantly be on guard. Movies, television programs and the music industry, to name just a few, all portray casual sex, and even unnatural sex, as acceptable and normal. Exposing ourselves to these media allows these sexual ideas to seep into our minds, and before long we, too, think of them as part of life.

Gradually the flesh begins to respond to these ideas and temptations, and we can become trapped in destructive patterns in a variety of ways. Take, for instance, pornography. Pornography is what happens when we take the sexual nature of people, a beautiful, creative and mysterious gift born out of God's perfect love, debase it to mere sensuality and exploit it for money. Through pornography, Satan uses our human sexual longings to trap us into bondage. It blocks the love of God that flows between husband and wife in the true and holy expression of our sexual nature.

In the last three years, I have ministered to three separate families whose lives have been devastated by the bondage of pornography. In two of the cases, young teenagers went into the family computer to work on school projects and found that their fathers had accessed pornography. One thirteen-year-old girl suffers depression over her shock and disappointment.

Other types of destructive patterns of behavior are evident in sexual addictions such as prostitution, adultery, incest, sexual abuse (either the abuser or the one being abused can live with ongoing destructive patterns) and homosexuality. All of these are explicitly condemned in God's Word, as they are contrary to His plan for marriage, a perfect and holy union ordained by Him (see Deuteronomy 27:20–23; Romans 1:24–27; 1 Corinthians 6:9–10).

God likens the marriage relationship to the relationship between Christ and the Church. Throughout Scripture, He calls Christ the "Bridegroom," and the Church His "Bride." If this is His picture of marriage, we must be that much more aware of the high regard in which He views it, and we must strive to make our marriages worthy of such a comparison. We cannot change our pasts, but we can ask the Lord to forgive our sins and to heal the wounds that those sins have left in their wake.

Sexual Abuse

Sexual abuse is not a sin on the part of the person being abused, but it needs healing just as much as the sinful areas that come about by choice.

I prayed with a man who, as an altar boy in his church, was continually preyed upon by his priest. The priest even touched him inappropriately while leading him in prayer to accept Jesus.

From a very young age, this lad had a deep love of God and a desire to serve Him. He also had deep needs for love and nurture because his father was unavailable to him. This combination created a deadly situation where this boy was an easy target. The inappropriate touching created tremendous confusion in his own sexuality, and for years he struggled with homosexual thoughts and feelings. After becoming a priest himself, it took many years of therapy, counsel and prayer to bring him into a place of wholeness.

Betty is another person who felt alienated from God and church. When Betty was 22 and just released from a mental hospital, my friend Ann Bauwens met her. Betty was sexually abused by her father from ages five through fourteen. Each night before he molested her, Betty's father would make Betty pray the Lord's Prayer with him.

Betty suffered with severe depression, alcohol abuse and promiscuity. Ann led Betty to the Lord in 1980, but Betty still had difficulty attending church because of feeling ashamed and guilty. Ann continued to extend the hand of friendship to Betty, loving her without judgment.

In 1987, when Betty and Ann were returning home from lunch one day, Ann felt led to share with Betty a teaching she had recently heard about cutting free from sexual partners. Betty immediately became interested, saying she was sure she needed this. Ann suggested that Betty say the first names of the men with whom she had been involved, and Ann would pray to sever any emotional or spiritual ties that still existed.

With tears in her eyes, Betty said, "Ann, you don't understand. There have been hundreds, many hundreds—perhaps thousands of men with whom I've been sexual."

Ann replied softly, "That's okay, Betty. God knows who they are." Ann proceeded to pray, separating Betty not only from her father, but from every other man with whom she had ever had an inappropriate sexual union.

At that moment, Betty said she felt a tremendous weight lifting up and off of her shoulders. She felt a lightness she had never experienced before. After this prayer of release, Betty attended church regularly for the first time in years, began reading the Bible and participated in a prayer group.

Homosexuality

Betty is not alone in her experience. Many people in our society today have had a great many sexual partners. This is not at all unusual for people who have been active in the homosexual lifestyle. They usually have a number of sexual partners throughout their lives. Anyone who has spent years ministering to people broken in this area will attest to this fact. Most homosexuals, particularly gay men, will admit that sexual promiscuity is common for those involved in the lifestyle.

171

There are two particular reasons that a homosexual union is an abomination to God. First, it is not biblical. In fact, it is contrary to what God's holy Word says about creation, love, marriage and sex. It twists what God intended to be holy and pure. Second, God's Word condemns it specifically (see Leviticus 18:22).

In actuality homosexual relationships are not as committed as people might think. Even when two homosexual men live together and think of themselves as a couple, it is rare that they are ever monogamous. The idea of a homosexual couple being exclusively committed to one another is a fallacy used to gain support for the acceptance of same-sex marriages.

Many years of my life have been spent working with and ministering to those struggling with the gay lifestyle. I have found that there are a number of possible components that can lead a person into homosexuality. It is so much more complicated than just "having a spirit of homosexuality," as some Christians believe.

Homosexuals usually become involved in the lifestyle out of unmet needs. Not receiving the necessary love and nurture as children creates a vacuum that propels many to make unhealthy choices in later life. All children need affirmation and acceptance from family members, and this is often shown through healthy physical touching like hugs, kisses, hand-holding or carrying a child on one's shoulders. Additionally, a child's confidence and self-image are created by extended family, teachers and other children. When these basic God-given needs are unmet, a void is created that lasts until these needs are fulfilled. Many people who enter the homosexual lifestyle are trying to fill these basic longings for love and nurture.

There may also be generational components in a family that has a history of unmet needs. A parent is unable to give love and nurture if he never received it himself. In utero wounding of rejection, judgment, fear or abandonment before the child is born, as we talked about earlier, could be involved. This often sets into motion a lifetime of neediness.

A lack of nurture from the same-sex parent may exist, or emotional, physical or sexual abuse may have taken place. A child learns his or her identity, sexual and otherwise, by emulating the same-sex parent or by same-sex adults around him. Occult involvement, as discussed in the previous chapter, may have opened spiritual doors in one's life. Remember, a person gets involved in the occult because he is trying to meet some of his own needs, often the need for power and control in some aspects of life.

And there may be the use of drugs and alcohol, along with a promiscuous lifestyle. This is often a result of trying to grasp physical or emotional comfort. Those unmet needs become less noticeable when numbed with drugs or alcohol, but, unfortunately, they only get worse.

Usually, homosexuality or promiscuity occurs because of a combination of all these possible reasons.

For further teaching on this topic I strongly recommend Francis MacNutt's book *Homosexuality: Can It Be Healed?*

Things to Remember When Praying to Be Cut Free

Regardless of how a person becomes involved in a promiscuous or homosexual lifestyle, he or she still needs to be cut free emotionally, spiritually, mentally and physically from all sexual partners. The ties created from sexual unions need to be broken. Furthermore, the ties created from all of the sexual partners that a person's partners have had need to be broken. The prayer should be for a cleansing and purification of the body, mind and spirit.

After the cutting free of unholy unions, there is usually a need for generational healing. This involves the cleansing of sexual sins passed down through the generations. Examples of these sins are family patterns of adultery, incest, pornography, sexual addictions or homosexuality. Many boys are introduced to pornography and prostitution by their fathers, who

173

think these are signs of manhood. Incest and homosexuality are two distorted expressions of love that not only persist but strengthen through the generations.

Another area that may need attention after cutting free of unholy unions is renouncement of occult practices. Some occult practices such as satanism and witchcraft involve sexual contact with a vast number of people, as well as group sex and bestiality. These practices are often done while under the influence of drugs and alcohol. All occult involvement needs repentance, as well as renouncement. If these practices have been passed down through the generations, again there is the need to include them in generational healing.

Finally, do not forget two important actions: the confession of sin and emotional healing. Emotional healing may involve prayer from conception to birth, as well as the healing of memories.

Inviting the Lord into memories of inappropriate sexual activity is vital. The Lord's presence brings peace, love and forgiveness into memories where the enemy has encouraged shame and guilt.

People are often embarrassed or ashamed to ask the Lord Jesus into these types of memories. I always ask the same question. I look deeply into the person's eyes and say, "Is this something the Lord Jesus doesn't know about?"

My question is usually met with a long pause as this truth enters the person's mind and spirit: Jesus knows everything, even the number of hairs on our heads (see Luke 12:7)! Remember—He comes to bind up the brokenhearted and to set the captives free (see Isaiah 61:1).

The Lord longs to come into all of our painful memories and to heal our shame and guilt and separation from God. Jesus was sent by God to do this very thing. Once the light of Christ comes into these dark and lonely places, filling them with His love and peace, a cleansing and purification of the body takes place.

174

And not only purification of the body; a cleansing of soul and spirit take place as well. After this, we are able to live for God in a newness and freshness never before experienced.

Shane was a young man I prayed with who was seduced and molested as a teenager by a teacher at a Christian school. He felt tremendous shame and guilt because his body responded sexually to the improper touching. He also struggled with sexual thoughts and feelings after physical education classes when showering with the other boys. This began a pattern of habitual masturbation.

After praying back through these memories and inviting Jesus into these places, Shane was able to release his guilt and shame. He saw and felt the Lord come into those situations and speak peace to his troubled spirit. Jesus spoke directly to Shane, telling him that the sexual body was created for the holy union of marriage. Shane said that in the healing of these memories, Jesus was able to communicate understanding, love and forgiveness to that young teenage boy who was still bound by the hurt.

By breaking free of unholy unions and experiencing emotional healing, new lines of communication open with the Lord. After Shane's inner healing, for instance, he began attending church, listening to and singing praise music all day every day. He also experienced a new oneness with his wife, physically as well as emotionally and spiritually. Spiritual intimacy with the Lord helps us better to understand and enter into the beauty and sanctity of the "holy unions" that God created for each of us. What a blessing!

Prayers for Cutting Free from Unholy Unions

Following is a prayer for cutting free from unholy unions that you may want to pray for yourself:

In the name of Jesus Christ and by the power of His cross and blood, I take the sword of the Spirit and cut myself free from all

175

previous sexual partners. I especially cut myself free from [use first names or initials only; don't worry if you cannot name them all, Jesus knows them].

I cut myself free from these people physically, spiritually, emotionally and mentally. I not only cut myself free from these people, Lord, but also from anyone and everyone with whom they have ever had sexual relations.

I place the cross and the blood of Jesus between myself and each of these people. I pray for a cleansing and purification of my mind, body and spirit, that I may walk in wholeness, purity and redemption.

Fill me with the power of Your Holy Spirit, that I may walk in Your abundant grace and mercy.

Fill me, Lord, with Your love, that it may permeate all the dark and lonely places. Most of all, Lord, help me to know how much You love me and how special I am to You.

I ask this in Jesus' precious name. Amen.

Following is a prayer you may want to pray for someone else:

In the name of Jesus Christ and by the power of His cross and blood, we take the sword of the Spirit and cut [name] free from all previous sexual partners. We especially cut [name] free from [use first names or initials only; don't worry if you cannot name them all, Jesus knows them].

We cut [name] free from these people physically, spiritually, emotionally and mentally. We not only cut [name] free from these people, Lord, but also from anyone and everyone with whom those people have ever had sexual relations.

We place the cross and the blood of Jesus between [name] and each of these people. We pray for a cleansing and purification of [name's] mind, body and spirit, that [he/she] may walk in wholeness, purity and redemption.

Fill [name] with the power of Your Holy Spirit, that [he/she] may walk in Your abundant grace and mercy.

*Fill [name], Lord, with Your love, that it may permeate all
the dark and lonely places. Most of all, Lord, help [name] to know
how much You love [him/her] and how special [he/she] is to You.
We ask this in Jesus' precious name. Amen.*

Cutting Free Emotionally from Unhealthy Relationships

In addition to unholy sexual unions, unhealthy relationships in general may need to be severed. These are relationships that have resulted in a soul-tie, or an unhealthy connection held by control or manipulation.

Soul-ties are created when we blindly follow someone and
allow him or her to make major decisions in our lives. If we
totally depend upon our parents, priest, minister, therapist or
doctor to make all of our decisions for us, or if we try to make
the decisions we think they would want us to make, we are
not learning to listen to God effectively, and we run the risk
of abuse, spiritual or otherwise.

When I was first introduced to the power of the Holy Spirit
and healing, I was constantly going to my father-in-law to
seek advice about what I should do in a particular situation.
Father Frank was such a wise spiritual leader. He would listen intently to everything I had to say and then he would pray,
"Lord, You know all there is to know about this situation
Norma's been talking about here. How about giving her some
direction about it, Lord? Oh, and Lord, thanks for listening
and helping us out."

Later, as I reflected on our meeting, I would realize that he
had not told me what to do. But somehow I felt better, and
when I thought about the situation again, I experienced peace
and direction.

By this type of relationship, my father-in-law taught me how
to hear and depend on the Lord, never allowing an unhealthy
dependency or soul-tie to be created between us. This is a style
of spiritual leadership that I have tried to emulate.

If we look at the life of Jesus, we see how He never allowed another person to control or manipulate Him. He did not allow the leaders of the day, or His disciples, or even His own mother to direct His beliefs or behavior. He did not allow Satan to manipulate Him through pride or fear. He listened to and obeyed the voice of His Father God. If we are following Jesus' example and trying to become more Christlike, how is it that we allow others to have control over our thoughts, feelings and actions?

I had a friend named Julie who put a lot of conditions on our friendship. If I did not respond to her the way she "thought I should" or "needed me to be," she wrote letters telling me I was not a good friend and had let her down. After a while I understood why none of her friendships ever lasted and why she was alienated from her family. Her expectations were too high, and being her friend felt too much like work. Feeling both smothered and judged whenever I was around her, and arriving home exhausted each time we were together, I eventually withdrew from this unhealthy relationship.

I prayed with a woman once who had to hide her car whenever she went to visit friends or family in a particular neighborhood because her best friend, Lucy, lived around the corner from them. Lucy would get upset when Renee spent time with anyone besides her and expected an accounting for her time. We are talking about adult women here, not insecure junior-high schoolgirls. These are both examples of unhealthy, dependent relationships.

When one becomes enmeshed or tied to another in this manner, unhealthy side effects can occur, such as a loss of one's individuality and self-confidence. Relying on another person besides God, or allowing that person to become an idol, is spiritually dangerous.

This can create further difficulties when a person is too dependent upon parents or family members. Real problems occur when the "controller" is a family member or an employer from whom you cannot totally sever all ties. This is where we have to try to be more like Jesus, who said: "Who is my mother, and who are my brothers? . . . For whoever does the will of my Father in heaven is my brother and sister and mother" (Matthew 12:48, 50).

As parents, we need to try hard not to control or manipulate our adult children and especially not to live their lives. We should have a listening and encouraging ear, without telling them what to do according to our beliefs or ideals. When my adult children say, "What do you think I should do, Mom?" I never say, "You should. . . ." I usually answer with this statement: "I have enough trouble living my own life—I can't live yours. But let's pray about it. God will tell you what to do." I encourage them, reminding them of good choices they have made in the past and how they should trust their own judgment. I brainstorm with them, looking at the pros and cons of the situation. I end by telling them I will continue praying for God's wisdom and direction in this matter.

This is much better than telling our children what to do, because I guarantee that if it does not work out, they will blame us. Unfortunately, it is human nature to blame others, especially when things go wrong or bad advice is given.

We so often hear the term *codependency*, referring to enmeshment or entanglement with another person in an unhealthy manner. My favorite definition of *codependency* is that when you die, another person's life flashes before your eyes! If we are this involved in another person's life, we are definitely not keeping our eyes on Jesus.

I have actually known and ministered to those who are so worried and concerned about a loved one that they become physically ill. This is when we have to "let go and let God." Only the power and love of God can change another human being. No matter how much we love and care about someone, Jesus loves and cares about him or her more. God has no grandchildren—only children.

This is where I find the opening lines of Reinhold Niebuhr's "Serenity Prayer" so helpful:

God grant me the serenity
to accept the things I cannot change;
courage to change the things I can;
and wisdom to know the difference.

Sometimes the only thing we can change is *our* attitude and judgments about a person or situation. And God is usually ready, willing and able to help us with these changes.

Think about your relationships. Would you consider them healthy or unhealthy? Do you think the Lord approves of them? Are there places where you are depending on another more than you are depending on God? Are there people in your life whom you control through guilt, shame, manipulation or fear? Are there people who control you through these same means? Are presents exchanged in your relationships with or without conditions? Do you like to remind others of how much you have done for them?

If you have answered yes to a number of these questions, you might want to pray one or both of the following prayers.

In the name of Jesus Christ, with the power of His cross and blood, I sever all unhealthy soul-ties with [name]. I ask forgiveness for allowing this relationship to develop into an unhealthy state.

I bind my heart and mind and soul to You, Lord Jesus, and to no one else. Place Your cross and blood between me and [name]. I pray that, where it is possible, You would salvage and rebuild the relationship into a healthy one, Lord, and where it is necessary, I pray that You show me the relationship that needs to be severed completely. I commit/recommit myself to You, Lord Jesus, and thank You for dying on the cross for my sins. I accept You and You alone as my Savior and Lord. Amen.

Or this one:

Lord Jesus, I ask forgiveness for the ways I have tried to control and manipulate others, especially [names]. I see this now as sin and seek your forgiveness by the blood of your cross. I recognize, Lord, that You are the Way, the Truth and the Life. I am not. I release my family, especially [names], into Your hands and I entrust them to You. I release my friends, especially [names], into Your hands and I entrust them to You. Please help me, dear Lord, not to try to take back control over them. Thank You, Lord, that You love them even more than I do. Thank You, Lord, that You can handle their lives better than anyone else, including me. Help me to completely entrust them to You. Amen.

PART THREE

WALKING
IN YOUR
HEALING

ELEVEN

THE IMPORTANCE OF LISTENING TO GOD

Have you considered the most unique aspect of man's existence in the Garden of Eden? It is that man and God were able to speak to one another. There was no communication gap. Man in his unadulterated, sinless nature was able to speak to God and also to hear God speak. Sin closed that open line of communication.

We learn from the Old Testament that God continued to speak to His people, but He no longer had direct give-and-take with each individual. Rather He communicated through the prophets, men and women who served as vital communication links. In fact, the position of these messengers was so key to Israel's relationship with God that any prophet who was considered to be speaking falsely was subject to death. The words they spoke from God were tested: If the prophecies came true, they were accepted and recorded, and the prophet survived; if the prophecy was incorrect or found to be false, the messenger was often stoned to death.

Thus, the world came to know that God had raised up the Hebrews and that they had a special covenant relationship with Him. It was into this family that His own Son would one day be born.

But for a time period of approximately four hundred years before the birth of Jesus, there were no prophets.

The Israelites had come to a place in which there was no communication with God at all. They could only look at what God had said in the past and wait expectantly for the new relationship prophesied of old in the words of the prophet Jeremiah:

> "The time is coming," declares the LORD, "when I will make a new covenant with the house of Israel and with the house of Judah. It will not be like the covenant I made with their forefathers when I took them by the hand to lead them out of Egypt, because they broke my covenant, though I was a husband to them," declares the LORD. "This is the covenant I will make with the house of Israel after that time," declares the LORD. "I will put my law in their minds and write it on their hearts. I will be their God, and they will be my people. No longer will a man teach his neighbor, or a man his brother, saying, 'Know the LORD,' because they will all know me, from the least of them to the greatest," declares the LORD.
>
> JEREMIAH 31:31–34

The great day came; the Messiah entered into the world and the *new covenant* was created:

> In the past God spoke to our forefathers through the prophets at many times and in various ways, but in these last days he has spoken to us by his Son, whom he appointed heir of all things, and through whom he made the universe.
>
> HEBREWS 1:1–2

We have seen that Jesus came to reveal God to us and to communicate His love for us. But we need to recognize that

186

He also came to reopen the lines of communication between us and God.

As Jesus said when praying to God the Father for His disciples: "Now they know that everything you have given me comes from you. For I gave them the words you gave me and they accepted them. They knew with certainty that I came from you, and they believed that you sent me" (John 17:7–8). Just as the disciples could relate to Jesus, talk with Him, share their concerns with Him, so, too, could they now relate to their Father in heaven.

This was not easy for them to understand at first. Look, for instance, at an earlier statement by Jesus: "I am the way and the truth and the life. No one comes to the Father except through me. If you really knew me, you would know my Father as well. *From now on, you do know him and have seen him*" (John 14:6–7, emphasis added).

Now look at Philip's response. I love this, because it is so human. Philip had traveled with Jesus, heard His teachings and seen His miracles. He had adjusted his entire lifestyle to follow Jesus, and yet he still responded, "Lord, show us the Father and that will be enough for us" (John 14:8).

Wouldn't you love to know what Jesus' tone of voice was like when He answered this? He said, "Don't you know me, Philip, even after I have been among you such a long time? *Anyone who has seen me has seen the Father*" (John 14:9, emphasis added).

So the disciples had difficulty understanding that Jesus was human but was God, and that He was sent to bridge the communication gap that had existed for millennia. This was something they understood more clearly after Pentecost when the power of the Holy Spirit came upon them and they found that they were once again able to communicate with God, this time through His Spirit. God truly wanted to communicate with His people then, and He still wants to communicate with us today.

187

If we are going to pray for healing, for ourselves and others, we must be able to hear His voice. As you will see from the examples in this chapter, obedience is a key part of learning to communicate. If we really want to hear Him, then He will help us learn how. Along with obedience comes discernment. We will also discuss certain methods for testing to make sure that the word you hear is really from God.

Learning to Communicate

Think of the people with whom you have close, personal relationships. You built those relationships and learned about each other by spending time together. For example, I spend a great deal of time playing and reading with my grandson, Andrew. As a result, I know which toys and books are his personal favorites. And after communing with my husband, Peter, for almost thirty years, I have learned never to discuss important matters with him until after he has had his dinner!

Communicating with God is like communicating with anyone: You both speak and you both listen. It is a two-way conversation, like on a telephone. Many people pray by going through a long laundry list of concerns. They never think of pausing to hear what God might want to say to them in return.

Our relationship with Jesus is usually what brings us closer to God the Father. As we read the Bible and hear and see what Jesus did in the gospels, we begin to feel a oneness with the Creator. We hear the Father speak and begin to understand His heart as we listen to Jesus' words and observe the miracles He performed.

It is rare to hear the Father speak audibly; generally, He puts His words into our minds. He gives us ideas that we know we did not generate on our own. The thought is given to us so clearly that we know it is from Him.

I recall with much joy this particular turning point in understanding in my own spiritual walk. When our son Jason was in the first grade, he was having trouble getting his schoolwork finished by the end of the day. I kept getting notes from his teacher that said Jason was not completing his assignments because he was daydreaming and looking out the window. As good study habits are developed early in a child's education, I was concerned. I was afraid that this would create a more serious problem down the road. I found myself wondering if God was interested in the smaller situations in our lives. I decided to try a little prayer experiment. I decided to pray every day about Jason's finishing his work at school.

This was a monumental decision for me, because previously I had only prayed about critical matters, like wars or cancer. I was under the false impression that God was very busy and that I should not bother Him unless it was an emergency.

I believe this false impression was the result of having five children and being somewhat limited at times in meeting all their needs. I had limited God by thinking of Him in human terms. I was not yet at the place in my spiritual walk where I realized that God is not only all-seeing and all-knowing, but He is also omnipresent. He is able to hear my prayers and communicate with me at the same time He communicates with others around the world.

So during my daily prayers I asked the Lord to help Jason finish his work at school. I did not tell anyone about this particular prayer, not my husband or prayer partner or anyone in my church.

About a month later, I was washing dishes at my kitchen sink and talking to my friend Beth, who was helping me part-time with my business. She and I often talked about spiritual things, and this particular day she asked me how I thought the Lord speaks to us. She wanted to know how I thought we could recognize the Lord's voice.

I answered, "Well, I think the Lord speaks to us in Scripture. You know those times when you are reading along and something leaps off the page, and you know it's just for you. I also think He speaks to us through others, like our priest or pastor during a sermon or a person who shares his or her testimony. He also speaks through books and tapes and music and especially those quiet times when we are truly listening to hear His voice."

"Do you think we should actually hear an audible voice," she asked, "or just an impression in our minds when Jesus speaks to us?"

"I'm not really sure," I said, "but I think Jesus speaks to us in a voice that we can individually understand."

During the last part of our conversation, Jason had come in from outside, all hot and sweaty from playing, and he was getting a Popsicle out of the freezer. Tugging on my skirt and looking up at me with his big hazel eyes, he said, "Mommy, sometimes I hear Jesus' voice."

Looking down, I responded, "You do, Jason? When do you hear Jesus' voice?"

He said, "I hear Jesus' voice when I'm at school and I'm looking out the window. He says, 'Come on now, Jason. Let's get this work finished. You can do it, Buddy.'"

And he ran out the door with his Popsicle, never realizing that his words had just changed his mother's entire prayer life. From that day on, I learned to pray and bring before the Lord all the things that were important to me and to listen for His answers. I learned that when we share our life with the Lord and ask Him to be a part of it, He will. In fact, it is what He has desired all along.

The Importance of Obedience

Thus, after learning to pray and invite the Lord into the everyday aspects of my life, I began trying to listen to His input. It is not easy to be still and listen to the voice of God. It is especially hard for us extroverts who spend much more time talking than listening. I am constantly reminding myself that

God gave me one mouth and two ears, and that perhaps this means that I am to listen twice as much as I speak.

One day I was still and listening and He spoke to me clearly. He said, *Norma, if you will listen, I will speak.* This was a very important word for me, but I believe it is a word for each of us. Scripture tells us: "Be still, and know that I am God" (Psalm 46:10). This is a discipline that takes both time and practice.

I learned to hear the voice of God through several personal experiences. Some of these experiences are amusing, while others caused me fear and embarrassment. But each of these situations taught me a great deal about faith in God and the importance of obedience.

After my husband and I became aware of the power of the Holy Spirit, we began trying to allow Jesus to become Lord over our lives. This meant to include Him in all aspects of our marriage and family at all times, as well as in our various professions.

This was not particularly easy, since up until this time we had been what I would call "Sunday Christians." My definition of a Sunday Christian is someone who knows Jesus as Savior, but has not invited Him into other aspects of his or her life, such as a profession, finances or leisure time.

About this time we were considering buying a used car. Peter had a friend at the bank who told him about a used Cadillac that had been repossessed. He suggested Peter take the car for the weekend.

On Friday, Peter brought the car home and we really liked it. As we were taking a ride that evening, I said, "You know, Honey, we are really trying to include the Lord in all areas of our lives, and this is a big financial responsibility. Don't you think we should pray and ask the Lord to guide us and tell us if this is a good car for our family?"

Peter said, "You're right. We really should pray." I'll never forget his prayer and its outcome as long as I live. He said, "Lord, we are really trying hard to hear Your voice about decisions in our lives. We aren't very good at hearing You yet, Lord.

191

We need a really big sign about whether to buy this car or not. Make it clear, please, Lord. Amen."

The next day, we were driving along in the car and the engine blew up! I mean, it *blew up!* We were unharmed and have laughed for years about how clearly God answered our prayer. We certainly had no doubts about whether to buy that car or not.

Another experience taught me a great lesson about listening to God. While driving down my street one day, I saw a neighbor in her yard planting a flower garden. I knew that her name was Nita and that she had children who attended the same local elementary school as my children, but they were in different grades.

As I drove in and out of our neighborhood over the next weeks, I found myself periodically checking on the progress of Nita's flower garden and meditating on Scriptures like Ecclesiastes 3:1–2: "There is a time for everything, and a season for every activity under heaven: a time to be born and a time to die, a time to plant and a time to uproot."

Often I observed her tending her garden, weeding, watering and fertilizing. I enjoyed the fruit of her labor. The beautiful array of flowers, with its riot of color, greeted me as I raced up and down the road attending to the business of my active life.

One day I felt an impression that I thought might be from the Lord. I felt as though He was saying, *I want you to write Nita a note and tell her how much her flower garden has blessed you and how you have experienced My creation in the beauty of it.* At first I thought, *No way. I can't be hearing this correctly.* Then, I began to hear it over and over again as I traveled up and down the street. The more I heard it, the more I argued with it.

I can't do it, I thought. *She'll think I'm a nut. I don't even know her.* After a while, as many of us do, I began to ignore the voice and the impression. It got to the point that I did not even look at the garden anymore because of the conflicting thoughts and emotions.

It was about this time that the Lord called my husband and me to move our family to England for a year, as I have mentioned elsewhere. We had much preparation to do before leaving—deal with our various professions, children's immunization records, passports, renting our home. The last thing I felt that I had time to do was write a note about a flower garden to someone I did not even know.

After moving to England and getting settled, I was praying one day and telling the Lord how I really wanted to walk in obedience to Him and be used to help His people. After a while, I heard Him say that if I was really sincere in this, why had I not written that note to Nita? I could not believe it! Here I was living across the Atlantic Ocean doing missionary work and I was still hearing about the flower garden back in Jacksonville, Florida.

I finally gave in and said, "Okay, I'll do it. But I still don't want to." I had to call a friend long-distance to get Nita's address, but I wrote the note. I started by saying I was sure she would think I was strange, but I really felt that God wanted me to tell her how much her flower garden had meant to me and how much I saw Him reflected in it. I will admit, I felt a lot of relief after I mailed the note.

A few months later, I traveled home for a week's visit to check on things and see my parents. During this time, I went by my home to visit with the renting family. Who do you think came jogging around the corner just as I was walking up to my door? You guessed it—Nita! She jogged over, stopped and said, "I thought you were living in England."

"I am," I answered. "I'm just home for a week."

I was so embarrassed, I could hardly look her in the face. But then she said, "I can't thank you enough for your note." And her eyes filled with tears. "I have to tell you something. I had decided not to plant my flower garden this year because it took up so much of my time. But when I got your note, I knew God was speaking to me. You see, when I work in my flower garden, that is my time with the Lord, when I really pray. I knew when I got your note that it was God's way of telling me He enjoyed our time together and that He really wanted to be with me. I'm certainly going to plant my garden again this year."

I was beginning to get the message, but He was not through with me yet. God gave me a third lesson in listening to Him.

One evening during choir practice, we were singing a beautiful song and I heard the Lord say to me, *Get up and tell Carter* [our choir director] *that this would be a good number for you to accompany with the flute.* This really frightened me because I am *not,* I repeat, *not* a good flute player.

The only reason I learned to play the flute at all was because it was a high school requirement that majorettes play an instrument. I had not even picked up my flute in years. In fact, I was not even sure I still had a flute.

By this time in my spiritual walk, however, I had grown a little in hearing the Lord and moving in obedience. And I knew that I could never in a million years have thought of playing the flute on my own. So during the break, I got up and said to Carter, "This would be a good number with the flute."

"What a great idea! I didn't know you play the flute," he replied. And before I could explain that I do not play well at all, he pulled me over to meet a young woman whom I had never seen before. With Carter's usual zest and enthusiasm, he said, "Norma, meet Jennifer. She just moved here, and she plays the flute, too! Why don't the two of you play a duet on this number in two weeks?"

Jennifer was excited about this idea, and we agreed to meet at my house several days later to practice. Frantically I dug out the flute and practiced a few scales.

When we met, we practiced for one hour and talked for two. Jennifer's husband was out on naval deployment for six months. They had just moved to Jacksonville, and she had no family or friends in the area. She had just started coming to our church in the hope of being part of a community.

Fortunately, Jennifer is a good flute player and she was able to carry the duet. We practiced with the choir and performed the duet during the offertory the following Sunday. I was astounded that I was not the least bit nervous, and I knew that this was definitely God's amazing grace.

After the service as I was leaving, I saw Jennifer sitting on the steps with her flute with an entire group of young girls sitting around her. She was playing different little tunes for them and letting each one try to play a note or two.

I just smiled as I walked by. I offered silent thanks to the Lord for using me to help Jennifer find her place in our church. She went on to play many more flute solos and to sing in the choir. She and her husband were active until he was transferred.

I have also learned a lot from my friend Emma, whom I mentioned in chapter 6. She is always listening to the Lord and obeying His instructions. She tries to keep the channel of communication open with God, seeking His face and praying, "Lord, how do You want to use me today? I'm available to be used. Help me to be a blessing to someone today."

God must really love this kind of prayer because He is *always* using Emma. She leads a most interesting and exciting life, and anyone who believes Christianity is boring has not spent much time with a person like Emma. If Emma cannot personally help you, she will get you to someone who can. She reminds me of the fellows who could not get their paralyzed friend in through the crowded doorway to see Jesus but, with faith and determination, carried him up onto the roof, dug through and lowered him into the room where Jesus was speaking. "When Jesus saw their faith, he said to the paralytic, 'Son, your sins are forgiven'" (Mark 2:3–5).

Emma is a wonderful example in my life of how God can use those who are listening for His Word, His leading, His direction in their lives. When we learn to listen to Him and then to obey Him, we are able to experience the joy and the privilege of sharing His healing touch with others. What a privilege this is!

Distinguishing God's Voice

When considering how to hear God's voice in prayer, the first question in most people's minds is, "How do I know this idea is from God?" How, indeed, do we know that an idea is not our own wishful thinking, the way we would like God to speak to us, or the enemy trying to mislead us? Several determining factors can help us in this discernment process.

First, does the message you are hearing line up with the Scriptures? Is what you are hearing something that can be substantiated by God's Word? If it is contrary to what the Bible clearly states as truth, reject it.

Once a woman came to me for prayer ministry and said she was hearing God tell her to divorce her husband of twenty years. She felt that God was telling her and her male therapist that they were to divorce their present spouses and marry each other. They believed that God was calling them into ministry together.

After I prayed, the Lord directed me to reach across and pick up the Bible that was lying on the table in my office. I handed it to her and said, "Can you please show me that in Scripture?" After looking at me for a long time, she finally whispered, "I can't." This threw the door open for her to recognize biblical truth. No longer was she deceived by the enemy, who clearly wanted to destroy the lives of two families.

Here is another factor that will help in discerning God's voice: Is the anticipated result of the message one that is consistent with the mind and heart of God as you know it? We see in the media how some radical fringe Christians actually believe they are doing the will of God by blowing up abortion clinics. How can they justify their actions with so many innocent people being killed? This in no way lines up with the new covenant that Jesus came to proclaim—God's tender mercy and salvation for every person.

"You have heard that it was said, 'Eye for eye, and tooth for tooth.' But I tell you, Do not resist an evil person. . . . You have heard that it was said, 'Love your neighbor and hate your enemy.' But I tell you: Love your enemies and pray for those who persecute you, that you may be sons of your Father in heaven."

MATTHEW 5:38–39, 43–45

It is critically important to be able to distinguish the voice of God from the voice of the enemy. Satan has great interest in interfering with our communication with God. He will do everything he can, however sneaky, to keep the Kingdom of God from advancing: He will impersonate God; he will use distractions and diversions to take our minds off the prayer conversation; he will inject himself and his words into the conversation. Remember how he tempted Jesus in the wilderness using Scripture? The enemy knows Scripture and can twist it, creating confusion and an inability to hear clearly. Never forget that he comes to rob, to kill and to destroy.

One of the best tools I have learned to use in my personal prayer life is to bind the enemy from interfering in my communication with God before I even enter into prayer. I begin with saying a short binding prayer, as we discussed previously in chapter 9. I pray something like this:

"In the name of Jesus Christ, with the authority given to me as a Christian, I bind all enemies of Christ. I bind anything that would try to interrupt or disrupt my hearing the Lord clearly or my prayer."

Next I pray for guidance by the Holy Spirit and that I will be able to hear the voice of God clearly. I then spend some quiet time simply entering into the presence of the Lord, usually picturing the face of Jesus. After this, with eyes closed, I try to listen to what the Lord wants to say to me.

Spending quality time in the presence of the Lord enables you to begin to recognize His voice more clearly. You begin to trust that what you are hearing is truly from Him. You also will begin to see the resulting fruit of your improved communication with God in your spiritual walk. After going through the process of listening, hearing, being obedient and then seeing good fruit, you begin to trust that you are hearing correctly. The more you experience this process, the easier it becomes to distinguish God's voice. No longer do you face the static or confusion that you once did. You are able to hear clearly and recognize the voice of God because you have spent time learning to listen and being obedient to His words.

In biblical times, when a shepherd tended his flock, he placed his sheep in a fold for the evening. The sheep were mixed in with a number of other sheep from other flocks. When morning came, the door was opened and the individual shepherd would call his sheep. Only the sheep belonging to that shepherd came out in answer to his voice. The sheep had spent so much time with their shepherd that they responded to him alone.

"The watchman opens the gate for him, and the sheep listen to his voice. He calls his own sheep by name and leads them out. When he has brought out all his own, he goes on ahead of them, and his sheep follow him because they know his voice. But they will never follow a stranger; in fact, they will run away from him because they do not recognize a stranger's voice."

JOHN 10:3–5

A New Relationship

In our relationship with God, we have come full circle from the Garden of Eden. Before sin, man was in direct communion with the Father and found conversation with Him a natural part of everyday life. When sin entered the picture, separating man from God, we were forced to rely on a few people selected by God as His spokespersons, as evidenced throughout the Old Testament.

For four hundred years after the death of the last prophet, man was isolated and could only rely on what God had said in the past, not what He would have us hear from Him in the present. Then Jesus came, and our new covenant relationship through Him—made permanent when God sent the Holy Spirit to dwell among us—reopened the direct channels of communication between the Creator and the created.

> Now there have been many of those priests, since death prevented them from continuing in office; but because Jesus lives forever, he has a permanent priesthood. Therefore he is able to save completely those who come to God through him, because he always lives to intercede for them.
>
> HEBREWS 7:23–25

Praise God for the new covenant, the restored relationship! May we come boldly before the throne with our requests and open our hearts—and ears—to hear.

TWELVE

THE IMPORTANCE
OF GODLY RELATIONSHIPS

Once a person experiences freedom through emotional healing, forgiveness and repentance, the importance of the relationship with God the Father and Jesus, His Son, becomes more fully understood. When the love and peace of Christ heal a person's deep wounds and when the power of the Holy Spirit is fully realized, the person's inclination is to share the good news with others. This is a natural part of the process and one that is quite scriptural.

God created each of us for union—union with Him and union with one another. We see this symbolically represented in the shape of the cross. The vertical beam points to our union with God the Father, and the horizontal beam stands for our union with one another. A right relationship with God frees us to have godly relationships with others.

People often ask, "How important is it to attend church?" Well, first, I believe it is important to recognize that a person does not have to go to church to be a Christian. Church is not what establishes the relationship with God. Rather, as we have discussed, we only come into a restored relationship with God through a personal commitment to and relationship with Jesus.

In fact, not everyone who attends church is a Christian. People often go for the wrong reasons. Some go to church for fellowship, business contacts, to hear good music, because they have done it their whole lives or because someone is dragging them there. It is wrong to assume that all churchgoers know Jesus on a personal level. I attended church for years and did not really know Jesus. The young man with AIDS whom I mentioned in chapter 2 regularly attended church but did not feel connected to Jesus in any way.

However, because it is God's plan for us to be in union not only with Him but also with other believers, He gives us the gift of Christian community. This community usually takes the form of church, but it also exists in other forms such as small support groups, prayer groups and Bible studies.

God gave us the gift of community because He wants us to be in union with one another, but also for a number of related reasons. First, Jesus Himself encouraged the community of believers, saying He would be with us when we gather in His name: "For where two or three come together in my name, there am I with them" (Matthew 18:20). There is no better reason to be involved in a Bible study, prayer group or Sunday school class than this. When two or more gather in the precious name of Jesus, He comes alongside us and He joins us. What a beautiful image, Jesus sitting among us as we pray and study the Scriptures!

Second, Jesus went regularly to the synagogue. We see this in the gospels where He picked up the scrolls and read that beautiful passage from Isaiah, often referred to as Jesus' "State of the Union" message:

He went to Nazareth, where he had been brought up, and on the Sabbath day he went into the synagogue, *as was his custom.* And he stood up to read. The scroll of the prophet Isaiah was handed to him. Unrolling it, he found the place where it is written: "The Spirit of the Lord is on me, because he has anointed me to preach good news to the poor. He has sent me to proclaim freedom for the prisoners and recovery of sight for the blind, to release the oppressed, to proclaim the year of the Lord's favor." Then he rolled up the scroll, gave it back to the attendant and sat down. The eyes of everyone in the synagogue were fastened on him, and he began by saying to them, "Today this scripture is fulfilled in your hearing."

LUKE 4:16–21, EMPHASIS ADDED

It was Jesus' custom and practice to go to the synagogue. If we are to pattern our life after His, then we, too, should regularly attend church.

Third, we attend church or Christian-related activities, such as a Bible study or small group, to gain knowledge and wisdom from those who are more mature in their Christian walks and to share knowledge with those who are not as far along. Each of us receives little glimpses of God on our journeys. We develop a more complete picture of God when we share with one another the insights we have received.

Sharing a small part of one's own life and struggles really can help another person. This is why support groups like Alcoholics Anonymous are so successful. People begin to feel hopeful when they hear about someone who has survived similar circumstances.

Fourth, we receive prayer support, another vital part of Christian community. Churches can be supportive in this regard, but smaller groups are often more effective in offering direct prayer support and in providing an open forum to talk about Jesus and to discuss spiritual questions.

At one time our church was divided into "growth groups" intentionally organized to include mature Christians, baby Christians and everything in-between. Everyone in these groups grew and matured from the insights and revelations shared by the other members.

Our first order of business in our weekly meetings was to pray for the needs of each member, focusing particularly on healing for the member or someone in the member's family. We had the unique blessing of walking one of our members through a serious bout with cancer. In addition, this group was instrumental in helping my husband and me prepare for our missionary sabbatical to England. Fifteen years after this group disbanded, we still feel a family kinship to its members and continue to follow them in their walks with the Lord, as they do ours.

In every small group there are occasions when a member is in such dire emotional straits that he or she is unable to pray. In such instances that member can be carried emotionally on the shoulders of the other group members. Even Jesus' disciples were instructed to go out in ministry two-by-two so they could support one another. We all go through spiritual deserts, "dark nights of the soul," when we need to be held up by our Christian family. We need to allow others to represent God's love, giving us hope and encouragement when we are unable to pray.

In addition to small group membership, it is particularly helpful to have a prayer partner, preferably of the same sex, who provides trust and confidentiality. I meet with my prayer partner weekly and can call on her more frequently if I need her. We are able to discuss and pray about things too intimate for large group discussion.

When I was a young mother with several children still at home, another young mother was my prayer partner. Lynn and I had much in common and could pray for our eleven combined children and our professional husbands. After entering ministry full-time, I found it particularly helpful to meet with Sue, who was also in a ministry and on staff at her church. We were and still are able to understand the necessary balance between ministry and personal activities. Even the year we lived in England, I found it helpful to have a prayer partner, Anne, who was also in full-time ministry.

The temptation is great in a large group setting to put one's best foot forward, seeking approval from people whose opinions we respect. In a small group context or with a prayer partner, however, a person can allow his or her true self to be seen without fear of judgment. Being able to confess sins in a safe environment and receive God's forgiveness is essential to emotional growth.

Prayer support is vital to each person's Christian walk and continual prayer for healing can be a significant part of that support. My husband meets in a prayer group with two or three other men weekly. The one other member who has been in this group for twenty years with Peter developed lymphoma in 1990. The group prayed for him at each meeting, and each man in the group interceded for him daily. He underwent a bone marrow transplant and several difficult weeks of hospitalization. At the writing of this book, he is the only person of his transplant group to have survived and he remains cancer-free.

The notion of praying for healing in Christian assemblies and Christian encounter groups is as old as the first-century Church. We looked earlier at the model for healing prayer that James provided:

> Is any one of you sick? He should call the elders of the church to pray over him and anoint him with oil in the name of the Lord. And the prayer offered in faith will make the sick person well; the Lord will raise him up. If he has sinned, he will be forgiven. Therefore confess your sins to each other and pray for each other so that you may be healed.
>
> JAMES 5:14–16

James' letter points out the importance of praying for healing for one another, but it also presents the fifth reason for Christian fellowship—accountability. We need to hold each other accountable for our actions in a forgiving and non-threatening environment, with godly admonition and without condemnation. It is Satan who condemns us and fills us with shame when we sin. God, speaking directly to us and through our Christian brothers and sisters, convicts without condemnation.

Finally, there is one last, and perhaps most important, reason that God calls us to community with one another. It is clear from Paul's letters that gifts of the Holy Spirit are not all bestowed on any one person. They are spread among the members of the Body in order to encourage a community ministry. "Now to each one the manifestation of the Spirit is given for the common good" (1 Corinthians 12:7). These various gifts of the Spirit are to be used in service to one another and in order to extend the Kingdom of God. Gifts such as prophecy, healing and miracles necessarily imply that they will be used in community. There is no place for these gifts in solitary Christianity.

Using one's gifts within the context of a Christian community, or the Body, is the purpose of the gifts themselves. "The body is a unit, though it is made up of many parts; and though all its parts are many, they form one body" (1 Corinthians 12:12). The various parts of the body are no good by themselves; they must work together in order to function as they were intended.

Jesus' parable of the man with talents is told in Matthew 25:14–30. The man who hid his talents, or gifts, in the ground was not rewarded because he did not use them as the giver intended. They did not benefit either the giver or the receiver because they were hidden away. If we hide our spiritual gifts, those precious gifts given to us by God our Father, we are, in essence, burying them in the ground. We must provide a way for them to be used in a Christian community in order for others and ourselves to be blessed by them.

My dear friend Cindy Farmer is one who has greatly benefited from the various gifts of many Christians. Her church family, friends, family, neighbors, Bible study groups and so many others have come alongside her and been her "community." I think you will agree after reading Cindy's testimony that "the manifestation of the Spirit is given for the common good" and various gifts of the Spirit are to be used in service to one another. I am confident you will agree after sharing Cindy's life that this courageous woman has truly "extended the Kingdom of God" not only by allowing others to minister to her, but by imparting hope, perseverance and a faith and trust in God that are unmatched.

The Testimony of Cindy Farmer

"I believe that I have been asked to contribute to this final chapter because my life literally plays out the previous chapters of this book. I *know* that I was created in the image of God for the purpose of communion and fellowship with Him. I *know* that my intended right relationship with Him was broken when sin entered the world at large and, thus, ruled my personal life. I *know* the depth of the Father's love that would give up His only Son as a perfect, unblemished sacrifice for my sins in order to restore that right relationship with the Father. I *know* He has empowered me with His Holy Spirit to be in constant communication with Him.

"Therefore I *know* I can pray, and He will hear and act. I *know* He will speak to me in ways I can understand and respond. How do I know that I know these things? The testimony and witness of my life explain how I came to have such assurance.

"The first seventeen years of my life were fairly ordinary by today's standards—two parents, two siblings, some good memories, some bad, and enough Christian education and influence to lead me into accepting that I was a sinner and needed a Savior, and that God had provided one. The next seventeen years were spent struggling to learn and live out the Word while attending college, teaching school and becoming a wife and mother of three boys. I tried to 'act' out my faith and pretended a lot of things were normal for appearance's sake, when I really did not have a godly marriage or family.

"Then, in an instant on an ordinary day, my family's life was turned upside down. I lost the control of our lives that I had fought so hard to maintain and began to understand James 4:14 when he says, 'Yet you do not know what your life will be like tomorrow. You are just a vapor that appears for a little while and then vanishes away' (NASB). I thought my tomorrows would continue as I had known them. Then my husband became the victim of a teenage drunk driver. He was left with a serious head injury, and my children and I experienced a total upheaval in lifestyle.

"After seven months of hospital care, my husband, with impaired functioning, returned home to a now unfamiliar and strained home atmosphere. I had spent those seven months juggling twice-weekly trips to the hospital (four hours away); being his emotional caretaker, trainer and cheerleader; raising our three boys alone (ages four months, four years and seven years); and living with constant stress, insecurities and fear. My body was beginning to show signs of a breakdown. Those signs increased and depression set in after another family tragedy occurred: My husband's dearly loved, elderly grandparents were both murdered by someone who broke into their home.

"My life seemed to continue in a downward spiral. I discovered certain information that proved how serious our marital problems were. To add insult to injury, I became the victim of physical abuse at the hands of an angry and frustrated brain-damaged husband and lived in fear for the safety of myself and my children.

"Then, when it seemed that nothing could possibly get any worse, I was diagnosed at the Mayo Clinic with a rare disease known as P.O.E.M.S. This is a multi-system autoimmune disease that causes nerve damage, muscle weakness, abnormal blood counts, legal blindness, skin changes and countless other symptoms. The prognosis is death in a few years. The various drugs that were used in an attempt to slow down the progression of the disease brought on numerous unpleasant side effects.

208

"During the year that all these events were taking place, I learned quite a lot about faith. All of my controlling, pretending, trying to 'keep it together' or even survive fell apart at the seams. In my state of feeling helpless, hopeless and 'healthless,' I found that many verses became real to me, verses like: 'Test yourselves to see if you are in the faith; examine yourselves! Or do you not recognize this about yourselves, that Jesus Christ is in you—unless indeed you fail the test?' (2 Corinthians 13:5, NASB). Jesus Christ had been in me since I was seventeen years old, but after years of learning, it was time to take the test of faith that life's circumstances had put before me.

"To use Norma's car illustration, it was time to invite Jesus to move from the passenger seat to the driver's seat. Switching seats did not prove to be an easy or quick transition for me. Basically, I was falling apart physically and emotionally. I was afraid of the future or lack of one. I wanted and needed a miracle.

"Someone told me about Christian Healing Ministries where Norma ministered at the time, and I was sure that was where I would receive an instant supernatural healing. It did not happen at the first visit, much to my disappointment. So I began going once a week for prayer ministry with Norma and her partner, my friend and driver, Emma. I also went another day a week for two hours of soaking prayer. Even though there is no known medical cure for my condition, Jesus spoke to me concerning my healing.

"He brought to my mind a vision of a totally wrecked car. He and I were standing there looking at it. Of course, I wanted a new one (my physical healing) and He said, *I could give you a brand-new one easily enough, but you would only wreck that one, too.* The verses that helped me to understand what Jesus wanted to do in and with my life were Psalm 107:19–20 (NASB):

> Then they cried out to the LORD in their trouble; He saved them out of their distresses. He sent His word and healed them, and delivered them from their destructions.

209

"The healing He had for me at this time was an inner healing, and it was accomplished by His Word—directly through Scripture and indirectly through the words of love and encouragement given by the many people He was placing in my life. But even after this inner healing, I struggled within myself. I was so depressed when I was not healed supernaturally that I was basically biding my time, waiting for (and worrying about) my natural death. In order to receive all the help and healing He had for me, like the Israelites, I had to make a choice.

"Deuteronomy 30:19–20 came alive to me:

> This day I call heaven and earth as witnesses against you that I have set before you life and death, blessings and curses. Now choose life, so that you and your children may live and that you may love the LORD your God, listen to his voice, and hold fast to him. For the LORD is your life, and he will give you many years in the land he swore to give to your fathers, Abraham, Isaac and Jacob.

"I deliberately and consciously chose life. That became the scarier of the two choices since by now I was divorced, diseased and financially destitute. How was I going to raise three boys as a single, handicapped mother with extremely limited physical, emotional and financial resources?

"The answer to that is what this chapter is all about—relying on and trusting God to meet your needs (see Matthew 6:33). I was not waiting to die any longer, and I could no longer wait for my circumstances to change so that I could live. It was time to begin to walk in my healing, which basically involved restoring and maintaining that right relationship with God by, in and through Christian community.

"Before I could begin to receive all the help and support God had for me, I had to get right with Him. The first thing that was required of me was fairly easy. I had to stay rooted in God's Word. I am a natural student who loves the Bible. I joined several Bible studies, read related books and maintained a fairly consistent personal study time.

"Many of my questions, doubts and fears were addressed specifically and directly in His Word. Studying God's Word helped me to stay focused on salvation, eternal life and receiving hope that God's peace, joy and comfort would return to my life: 'May the God of hope fill you with all joy and peace as you trust in him, so that you may overflow with hope by the power of the Holy Spirit' (Romans 15:13). But when and how I could experience this hope was still a mystery.

"At that time, my inclination was to hide in a quiet corner somewhere and lick my wounds. Fortunately for me, there was no quiet corner in a home with three growing boys. It was a constant verbal barrage: 'What's for dinner?' 'Where are some clean socks?' 'I don't feel so good' (sounds following that cannot be described here). 'He did it.' 'Did not!' 'My teacher wants to talk to you.' 'My coach needs ten quarts of Gatorade.' 'Got milk?' Dog barking, phone ringing, TV blaring, music playing.

"These sounds were interspersed with a refrain playing over and over in my head: First, *Help!* Then, *Somebody help me!* And finally, *God, help me!* When I finally got around to calling on His name, He was faithful and true to answer.

"He directed me to the next step in helping me find healing and wholeness—a right relationship with others. This was a huge undertaking for me, as well as my prayer ministers, Norma and Emma. We started with all past relationships—parents, siblings, husband, in-laws and friends. We examined and prayed about them one at a time. Since I had been so deeply hurt and wounded, the main issue was obvious: *forgiveness.*

"Forgiveness was tricky because I had been raised to be a peacemaker and caretaker, and I achieved this by suppressing anger. So first, I had to recognize and admit that I was mad and angry. And to do that, I had to believe that I was a beloved child of God, created in His image and worthy of being loved and treated well by others.

211

"I learned that admitting my pain and forgiving the one who caused that pain (whether it was another person, my own self or even God), actually allowed God to work in my life by placing me deep within the Christian community, the true family of God, where I began to receive showers of blessings. Let me explain what I mean.

"In my weekly sessions with Norma, I was learning how unforgiveness can block the blessings God wants to give us. On one particular Monday, I started my session whining and complaining about various things I could not do for my boys. 'Norma, the boys haven't been to the dentist in two years because I have no dental insurance and no money to pay for checkups. And I know that as soon as I do get them to one, I'll be told that Daniel needs braces. I can't afford to meet my kids' basic needs, much less anything fun or extra. They will never get to go to Walt Disney World like other kids.'

"Norma responded as she frequently did, 'Have you prayed about it?' Much as I hated to admit it, my usual answer was no, and this day was no different. Since we usually prayed at the end of each session, we went on to deal with the relationship of the day.

"On this particular day the Holy Spirit softened my heart and I was able to forgive a relative and cut myself free from that destructive relationship. I had thought I needed him in my life for financial reasons, but it became clear in that session that he used money to control me. After this inner healing and prayer, I left Norma's office spiritually and emotionally richer, but no better off financially.

"I went home and read Isaiah 55:8: '"For my thoughts are not your thoughts, neither are your ways my ways," declares the LORD.' I submitted to letting God solve my problems His way and felt free—released from the bondage of false security.

"That was Monday night. At eight o'clock Wednesday morning, I received a call from a woman I had met at a luncheon two weeks before. She began by saying she hoped I did not mind but she had told her husband about me and my boys. She went on to say her husband was a dentist and would like to offer his services for free. I stammered in disbelief before gratefully accepting and setting up appointment times. I had not known he was a dentist, much less a Christian one with a servant's heart.

"At eight-thirty I got a call from a friend who said she had taken her daughter for a routine visit to the orthodontist and told him about Daniel's needing braces. This wonderful Jewish man offered to fit Daniel with braces and follow up with him monthly for the necessary two to three years. My disbelief turned into awe. Every time Daniel smiles with beautiful, straight teeth, I am reminded of God's care and concern for all the details of our lives.

"At nine o'clock I received my third call that morning. It was from a friend and neighbor who is a nurse. She explained she could get specially priced tickets to Disney World through her hospital, and she would like to take us that next week. I hung up the phone and shouted, 'We're going to Disney World! Thank You, God!'

"Truly no human could ever plan and provide for us the way God does. The 'Wonderful Wednesday' that left me awestruck has become a daily occurrence of miraculous answers to prayers. God uses many people and events to keep me and my family moving in His direction and at His speed. Sometimes He meets our needs in conventional ways using obvious Christian servants. Other times He uses unconventional ways and highly unlikely means of delivering His care and blessings. The point is: Any area of my life that I am willing to submit to Him, He will use to bring me closer to Him and bring glory to His name. Does this mean He makes my life perfect here on earth? No, it means He makes it perfectly okay to live out my unique set of circumstances while here on earth as He leads me into eternity.

"For example, I currently receive no SSI, disability, Medicaid, welfare or food stamps. (Not that these are wrong— God is just not using them in my life at this point.) I am not employed, so I have no steady income. Yet solely by the love and grace of God—and the members of His Body who are in touch with His loving heart—I live in a comfortable home, have nice clothes and eat well. I have vacationed at the beach, gone on retreats in the mountains and even taken a cruise to Mexico!

"My youngest son is in private school, and my eighteen-year-old is in college. He and his older brother own their own cars, and all three children have enough name-brand clothes and shoes to feel comfortable among their peers. None of these things in and of itself is important. The fact that the Lord loves me, listens to me and responds to my prayers is what is important.

"Beyond finances, God is constantly at work in my physical wellbeing. Did He cure the P.O.E.M.S. and restore my body to a healthy state? No, but He has kept me alive years longer than predicted, years longer than others with this disease have lived.

"And what about the quality of life when you deal daily with a chronic illness? Through His great mercy, He enables me to do what I can and sends help to do the rest so that I lead a full, productive and satisfying life. My home has many handicap features that enable me to be independent. My shower was paid for by friends. My electric wheelchair was prayed in by Norma, and my manual wheelchair and walker were found at a garage sale. My travel chair was donated by friends. Ramps in my home were built by church youth. The list goes on and on and on. With the help of many drivers—retired persons, homemakers, other moms and teens—I go to my children's sports events and school functions, run errands and basically live a pretty normal life in spite of some pretty abnormal circumstances.

"I have health insurance and a wonderful team of doctors at the Mayo Clinic. I take quite a few prescription drugs, but God has protected me from many of the devastating side effects. He gives me relief from fatigue, pain and discouragement in many varied ways for which I am so grateful. I have learned to thank Him in the midst of the dark moments, and I have found those moments to be shorter and shorter in duration.

"When my heart is filled with thanksgiving, it overflows to others. I have had many opportunities to share my story. Every time I am able to tell of God's faithfulness, it builds my faith. I continue to pray for complete physical healing. However, while I am no longer waiting to die, I am no longer waiting for a total healing in order to live. I am living out my unique circumstances by the grace of God, for the will of God and with the help of God and all the people, things and events He puts in my path. I am walking in the healing He has given me, with the Christian community He has provided to walk through it with me.

"This brings me to the final and most important area of my life in which God is continuously answering prayers—the spiritual. For now one of my theme verses is: 'Therefore, if anyone is in Christ, he is a new creation; the old has gone, the new has come!' (2 Corinthians 5:17). All the events of life have taken me to new and deeper levels of loving God, others and myself. That is really what life is all about—*love*. Jesus said to love God with all your heart, soul and mind and to love your neighbor as much as you love yourself (see Matthew 22:37–39).

"It is like knowing a secret or solving a mystery when we realize that true happiness and real joy do not come from good health or great wealth but from being in His presence. Whatever it takes to get to that place is worth it. Each day brings me closer to Him, and the joy I have now is full and complete."

In Conclusion

Cindy's testimony may be the best example I know of a person who has experienced the healing power of the one true God and who walks in that healing daily within the Christian community, or Body, that God has given her. This is where God wants us to be. He does not want us to be perfect by the world's standards—perfect body, perfect job, perfect family, perfect home. He wants us first and foremost to be in a healed relationship with Him. Then He wants us to heal our relationships with others and with ourselves. Finally, He wants us to live out that healing daily by growing closer to Him and closer to those Christians He puts in our lives. This is God's model of perfection—the model exemplified by the life of Jesus.

And in emulating Jesus, we go alongside one another, extending the healing hand of God to those in need, regardless of our differences. We are brothers and sisters in Christ, gathering around one another for healing prayer.

Loving God first and one another second—this is the transformation needed for living an abundant life in Christ. "All the Law and the Prophets hang on these two commandments" (Matthew 22:40).

As we follow these commandments and begin to live and move and have our being in God, we become more like Jesus, reaching out to a broken world with love and in peace. We are able to extend to others what has been extended to us— love, mercy and grace. We are able to receive healing from God, and then to pass this same healing along to others, reaching out the hand of God to one another—reaching out with the healing touch.

216

Suggested Reading List

Part 1: Healing Our Relationship with God

A Stranger to Self-Hatred: A Glimpse of Jesus, Brennan Manning (Denville, N.J.: Dimension Books, Inc., 1982)

About God and You, Father Frank Dearing (South Plainfield, N.J.: Bridge Publishing, Inc., 1982)

How to Pray for the Release of the Holy Spirit, Dennis Bennett (South Plainfield, N.J.: Bridge Publishing, Inc., 1985)

Part 2: Practical Tools for Healing

An Invitation to Healing, Lynda Elliott (Grand Rapids: Chosen Books, 2001)

Blessing or Curse: You Can Choose, Derek Prince (Grand Rapids, Mich.: Chosen Books, 1990)

Deliverance from Evil Spirits, Francis MacNutt (Grand Rapids, Mich.: Chosen Books, 1995)

Forgive and Forget, Lewis Smedes (New York: Pocket Books, 1984)

From Generation to Generation, Patricia Smith (Jacksonville, Fla.: Jehovah Rapha Press, 1996)

Healing, Francis MacNutt (Notre Dame, Ind.: Ave Maria Press, 1999)

Homosexuality: Can It Be Healed? Francis MacNutt (Jacksonville, Fla.: self-published, 2001)

Praying for Your Unborn Child, Francis and Judith MacNutt (New York: Doubleday, 1988)

Restoring the Christian Family, John and Paula Sandford (Tulsa, Okla.: Victory House, Inc., 1979)

The Believer's Guide to Spiritual Warfare, Thomas B. White (Ann Arbor, Mich.: Servant Publications, 1990)

Part 3: Walking in Your Healing

About God and People, Father Frank Dearing (Jacksonville, Fla.: Christ Counsel, 1983)

Healing Prayer: Spiritual Pathways to Health and Wellness, Barbara Shlemon Ryan (Ann Arbor, Mich.: Servant Publications, 2001)

Sacrifice of Praise, Ann Smith (Belleville, Ontario: Guardian Books, 2000)

The Prayer That Heals, Francis MacNutt (Notre Dame, Ind.: Ave Maria Press, 1981)

The Sword of the Spirit, The Word of God—A Handbook for Scriptural Intercession, Joy Lamb (Jacksonville, Fla.: Lamb Books, Inc., 1993)

Many of these books may be ordered with check, cash or credit card through <www.healingtouchministries.com> or by writing The Healing Touch, P. O. Box 7117, Jacksonville, FL 32238-7117.

INDEX

Norma Dearing is executive director of Impact Communications Ministries in Jacksonville, Florida, the non-profit Christian organization that produces the radio program *The Healing Touch*. Norma is the featured speaker on this program that teaches the biblical message of the healing power of Jesus.

Norma speaks internationally about prayer for healing and trains individuals and church groups in the areas of healing prayer and evangelism. For many years, Norma served as a prayer minister with her father-in-law, the late Rev. Frank Dearing, an Episcopal priest and pioneer in the healing ministry. She also served as director of prayer ministry at Christian Healing Ministries for fourteen years with Francis MacNutt, during which time she developed the School of Healing Prayer, Levels I, II and III, as well as the Foundations of Healing Prayer courses.

She and her husband, Circuit Court Judge Peter Dearing, have traveled to England twice to conduct healing missions in Leeds and Guildford. In 1984, Peter and Norma, together with their five children, served as missionaries in England. In England, the Dearings were guest speakers and ministers in eighteen different churches. They also began a street evangelism ministry of "board painting" and preaching the Gospel, building a team of more than thirty people in Guildford to carry on this work.

Norma is a member of the Order of St. Luke. She was graduated *magna cum laude* from the University of North Florida with a degree in psychology and was selected as one of the Most Outstanding Women of America. In addition to being a mother of five, Norma is grandmother of three.

For further information regarding *The Healing Touch*, please contact the ministry at P.O. Box 7117, Jacksonville, FL 32238, or find us on the Web at